Questioning
Your Way
to Faith

"Who is God? Why am I here? Where are we going? If you have questions about the Christian faith or if you have friends with questions, you are not the first and won't be the last. This book will help you process your concerns with compassion and truth. Whether you are curious about the Christian faith or you are rock solid in your beliefs and want to help someone know Jesus, pick up *Discover* and encounter the beauty and wonder of the Christian gospel that has given hope to believers for 2,000 years."

> **Daniel Darling,** Director, The Land Center for Cultural Engagement; bestselling author of several books, including, *The Dignity Revolution, A Way with Words,* and *The Characters of Christmas*

"As the parent of two teens, as a pastor, and especially as a former teenage questioner who was afraid to express my uncertainties, I am deeply grateful for Mike McGarry's new book. I love that *Discover* does not underestimate the minds and abilities of teens to think through and to grasp wonderful truths about God and his Word. This is just the kind of resource parents and youth ministers should have on hand to shepherd the next generation toward a deep, affectionate, and rich relationship with Christ."

> **Barnabas Piper,** Pastor, Immanuel Church, Nashville, TN; author of *Help My Unbelief*

"In a day and age when we are encouraged to embrace a personally-formed spirituality without regard to theology, we must recognize that any God-talk or engagement with the Christian faith is *all* about theology. Everyone is a theologian. It's simply a matter of un-intentionally doing theology poorly, or intentionally doing theology well. I'm grateful that Mike McGarry has given us a tool to use with our students that respects their ability to go deep, offers sound biblical theology, and can be used by both youth workers and parents to spark solid theological thought and discussion that will serve to build up students for a lifetime of faithfully following Jesus."

> **Walt Mueller,** President, Center for Parent/Youth Understanding

"As a youth pastor at my church for almost thirty years, as well as a professor of youth ministry, I will use and recommend this book enthusiastically. Mike suggests that students can read this book with a mentor or adult leader or in small groups, but I would love to buy this book and give it away to every student I could. There is also immense instructional value for small groups, student leadership teams, or one-on-one discipleship of students, to help grow their faith and transform their lives."

    Danny Kwon, Pastor of Youth and Families, Yuong Sang Church; adjunct professor, Eastern University/Missio Seminary; author of *Mission Tripping* and *A Youth Worker's Field Guide to Parents*

"Today's teens grow up in a confused and skeptical world. Mike McGarry gives pastors and churches a tool that doesn't shy away from hard questions but instead roots students in biblical truth. *Discover* will be a great resource for youth pastors preparing kids for baptism or confirmation."

    Jared Kennedy, Editor, The Gospel Coalition; author of *The Beginner's Gospel Story Bible* and *Keeping Your Children's Ministry on Mission*

DISCOVER

DISCOVER

Questioning Your Way to Faith

Mike McGarry

New
Growth
Press

newgrowthpress.com

New Growth Press, Greensboro, NC 27401
newgrowthpress.com

Cover Design: Faceout Books, faceoutstudio.com
Interior Typesetting and eBook: Lisa Parnell, lparnellbookservices.com

ISBN: 978-1-64507-353-6 (Print)
ISBN: 978-1-64507-354-3 (eBook)

Library of Congress Cataloging-in-Publication Data

Names: McGarry, Mike, 1980– author.
Title: Discover : questioning your way to faith / Mike McGarry.
Description: Greensboro, NC : New Growth Press, [2023] | Audience: Ages 12–18 | Summary: "Mike McGarry explores the twenty most common questions teenagers ask and how to see these questions as an opportunity to dig deeper and grow in faith"— Provided by publisher.
Identifiers: LCCN 2023000768 (print) | LCCN 2023000769 (ebook) | ISBN 9781645073536 (print) | ISBN 9781645073543 (ebook)
Subjects: LCSH: Christianity—Miscellanea. | Teenagers—Religious life.
Classification: LCC BR121.3 .M328 2023 (print) | LCC BR121.3 (ebook) | DDC 234/.23—dc23/eng/20230329
LC record available at https://lccn.loc.gov/2023000768
LC ebook record available at https://lccn.loc.gov/2023000769

Printed in Canada

30 29 28 27 26 25 24 23   1 2 3 4 5

For the teenagers
at South Shore Baptist Church

Contents

Acknowledgments

I received my copies of *Lead Them to Jesus: A Handbook for Youth Workers* while hosting a service week for the students in my ministry. Naturally, I was excited to get my box of books. A group of students gathered around while I beheld that beautiful turquoise cover for the first time. A few of them flipped through the book, and when they saw that the first section addressed common theological questions students ask, they said, "Hey, I'd read this." And that's how this book came about.

Thanks to Sarah and Brooke for accidentally giving me the idea to rewrite that first section into its own book, and thanks to Barbara Juliani and the rest of the team at New Growth Press for their support for this project. I'm also particularly thankful to Pastor Cody Busby for his leadership and support as my pastor at South Shore Baptist Church. And to my Youth Pastor Theologian family, you give me hope that there's a bright future ahead for youth ministry.

The biggest thanks belongs to my family. Tracy, you are my rock and greatest supporter. Matt and Hannah, you make my life richer and give me great joy.

Introduction

Teenagers ask great questions. When I think about the most difficult questions I've been asked in nearly two decades of youth ministry, they're usually prefaced with, "So, I know this is a stupid question . . ." or "I feel like I should already know the answer to this question, but . . ." and then they ask a nuanced theological question that's been debated by the greatest theologians and philosophers for two thousand years. And it's not just upperclassmen. Many of those questions come from the same middle school boys who refuse to admit they got hit during dodgeball and whose body odor makes youth leaders second-guess their commitment to youth group. But that's the beauty of helping young people discover faith: you never know what's going on in students' heads until you make it okay to ask their questions.

I sincerely pray this book is an opportunity for you to discover faith by leaning into your questions. Maybe you've grown up in church and haven't felt comfortable enough to ask your questions. Perhaps doubts have crept in that you're having a hard time admitting even to yourself. Or maybe you're new to Christianity and have some questions about what it really means to follow Jesus. I'm also hoping that some of you readers are young men and women who don't consider yourself a Christian, but you're interested in learning how Christians respond to these common questions. Whoever you are, and whatever the reasons you have for reading this book, I'm praying for you, and I hope this book helps you believe that the gospel really is the good news of great joy for all people.

There are three different ways you can choose to read this book: on your own, with a parent or mentor, or with a small group. The "Digging Deeper" section at the end of each chapter includes a few reflection questions. If you're reading on your own, you can write in the book or in a journal as you process each chapter's message. If you're reading with others, use these questions to discuss and to learn from each other. I'll admit that I often skip over discussion questions when I read them in other books, so if you do the same, I get it. But they're there, so you might as well give them a chance to help you process what you've read. You're reading the book—so make the most of it by really chewing on it before getting sucked back into your phone and homework. Read the questions and take a few minutes to discuss or write down a short response before moving on.

1
What Is the Gospel?

The gospel is the best news in the history of creation. And yet, many who've grown up in church are so familiar with some parts of the gospel they've stopped listening to it. Even though some could repeat the Sunday school definition, "gospel means 'good news,'" most will struggle to articulate what that good news actually is. Since the gospel is the heartbeat of this entire book, it's important for us to begin by getting clear on what the gospel really is.

GETTING CLEAR ON THE GOSPEL

The gospel isn't a good idea or a mystery that we need to unlock. The gospel is a person: Jesus Christ. He is the "good news of great joy for all people" that the angels declared when they announced his birth (Luke 2:10). The gospel is good news because it's a celebration of who Jesus is and what he has done to save sinners and adopt them as children of God through the power of the Holy Spirit. In this sense, the gospel isn't merely news to tell, it's an invitation: "Here's who God is and what he's done to make us his dearly loved children." If it's true, it's a message worth shouting from the rooftops.

It is impossible to receive the gospel in faith without believing in these key components: Jesus's sinless life, atoning death, and victorious resurrection. Who Jesus is matters just as much as what Jesus did. Jesus lived a sinless life, died a painful death as the substitute for all of God's children, rose from the grave in victory over sin and death, and will return to complete both his judgment of sin and the salvation of his people. This is good news for every generation, and it is worthy of being proclaimed every chance we get.

There are times I've heard "the gospel" preached with barely any mention of Jesus. That's not the gospel, even if those sermons included gospel-sounding promises. The gospel is good news about Jesus. In many ways, Jesus actually *is* the gospel. The gospel is not a set of theological beliefs or a spiritual mystery that needs to be unlocked. Talking about the love and grace of God is not the same thing as believing the gospel. After all, faithful Jews and Muslims can talk about God's love!

At its heart, the gospel is the proclamation that God saves sinners through Jesus Christ. It is not a "new law" or an update to the Ten Commandments. It is the grace of God that sinners receive by faith in who Jesus is and what Jesus has done. If we overlook or downplay the bad news of sin and judgment, then the gospel becomes much easier to shrug at. The gospel is good news of great joy because there is bad news: the wages of sin is death, and we're all guilty (Romans 3:23, 6:23). Through the gospel, sinners can become children of God, be set free from bondage to sin and guilt and shame, and have a new destiny: eternal joy in the presence of God, their heavenly Father. This, my friends, is good news indeed!

The gospel of grace lies at the heart of Christianity. We live in a world that puts so much pressure on you to get good grades, earn that scholarship, and change the world. But Jesus simply invites you to come to him. You don't need to be impressive or worthy. You don't need to clean yourself up before God will accept you. The Bible says it this way, "But God shows his own love for us in that while we were still sinners, Christ died for us" (Romans 5:8). This gift of grace is just that, a gift. It's unearned, undeserved, and doesn't need to be paid back. Believing the gospel will change your life because when you turn away from sin in order to follow Jesus, then God will transform you from the inside out (instead of requiring you to fix yourself on the outside before he "moves in").

TWO WAYS WE MISUNDERSTAND THE GOSPEL

There are two approaches to the gospel that I believe need to be revisited: one that crams Jesus down people's throats, and another that attempts to "preach the gospel without words." Although they appear to be opposite approaches, they are actually different sides of the same coin. Both try to compel a genuine profession of faith. This means that, at best, these approaches only produce false converts who conform to the externals of Christianity for a while.

The force-feeding approach fails because we're all the same in this regard: when someone crams something down your throat, you're probably going to vomit it out even if it's good for you. We know this, but some youth workers and parents continue to do it anyway. Many church kids have not rejected Jesus as much as they've rejected him being forced upon them through pressure to think and behave like a Christian without their heart being in it. Their parents and youth workers misunderstand the gospel because good news of great joy doesn't need to be forced; it simply needs to be announced. The gospel takes root in the heart before it changes anyone's behavior. Consider your own background and prayerfully reflect on whether your faith is the result of your own relationship with Christ or if it's the result of your parents' (or youth leader's) desire for you. My prayer is for this book and the "digging deeper" questions to prompt you to question your way toward faith.

The "preach without words" approach falls short because none of us can *be* the gospel. The gospel is an announcement. It tells of God's grace poured out on sinners through the life, death, resurrection, and eventual return of Jesus Christ. When Christians live in a way that reflects the gracious love of God, it may warm nonbelievers toward hearing the gospel, but they still need to *hear* it, because it's news about *who Jesus is and what he's done*—not about what we have done to love them. So, let's drop the talk about "being the gospel" and be free from that kind of pressure—who can live up to that? Instead, let's walk by faith as we are being changed by the gospel, loving others as Christ loved us, and telling them what God has done through Jesus. As we do these things, the gospel will be heard and its power to change lives will be seen.

THE GOSPEL IS FOR CHRISTIANS TOO!

The gospel is so much more than just a message that calls sinners to trust in Jesus for salvation and new life. The gospel of grace lies at the heart of our *whole* salvation: justification (our righteous standing with God), sanctification (our growth in holiness), and glorification (our coming perfection). And yet, with sanctification, it is common for Christians to overlook the centrality of the gospel. It can seem like what we need most is practical advice about how to become more like Christ. This usually happens with good intentions, but it leads believers into works-righteousness (believing our good works contribute to our justification) rather than daily dependence on the Holy Spirit. As the apostle Paul cries out in Galatians 3:3, "Are you so foolish? Having begun by the Spirit, are you now being perfected by the flesh?" Justification, sanctification, and glorification all rely on faith and grace, not on human effort.

Theologians often refer to four chapters of salvation history: creation, fall, redemption, and glorification. This is helpful to remember because it lets us locate where we are in our walk with Christ. Of course, none of us are still in the creation chapter, and no one alive has already been glorified. So everyone you meet is marked by either the fall or redemption. Those who have not professed faith in Christ and repented of their sin are still marked by the fall—they do not belong to Christ and they need to hear and believe the gospel. But those who have confessed their sin, confessed Christ Jesus as Lord, and have professed their desire to turn from sin and follow Jesus (repentance) are marked by redemption. They have been transformed by the grace they received and by the power of the indwelling Holy Spirit as they hear and grow in the gospel. This is why the gospel is the heartbeat that drives everything about our relationship with God.

Many teenagers who grow up in the church seem to talk about the gospel from their heels, holding back from believing it with joyful enthusiasm because they aren't sure it's all that great. Do you really believe the gospel is good news of great joy, or do you think it's just okay? Is your heart bored or lukewarm toward the gospel? The single best thing you can do for your life is to continually warm your own heart by the life-giving message of the gospel. If the gospel is just okay news, then it's on a level playing field with any number of other life-improving philosophies. But if it's true that God really does save sinners through Jesus, and that it's all a work of grace, then it really is good news!

DIGGING DEEPER

Use these questions for your own personal reflection and journaling, or for discussion with others.

- What does the author mean by saying, "The gospel is not a good idea?" What are some ways we can reduce the gospel to being just that?
- Based on this chapter, how would you describe the gospel in one or two sentences to a friend who asked?

- What are some common ways you've heard others misunderstand the gospel?
- What are the four "chapters" of salvation and how does that help Christians make sense of the world and the future?

2
Can I Be Sure of My Salvation?

The gospel is the proclamation of the good news that God saves sinners through Jesus Christ. An undeniable part of this message is the invitation to come and be saved. But what does that mean, and how can Christians be assured of their salvation?

Not every Christian knows when they became a Christian, and that's okay. Some people can tell you about the exact moment when they placed their faith in Jesus Christ; others came to faith over a period of time (often as children who grew up in church) and can't identify when they first believed the gospel. Following Jesus is about more than a singular moment when you pray a prayer; it's about living as a dearly loved child of God who has received grace through faith in Jesus who lived, died, rose again, and will return one day. It is important to be clear on what it means to be a Christian, so you can rest on God's promise when doubts creep into your heart and mind.

COUNTING THE COST
Becoming a Christian is the best decision you could ever make. I highly recommend it! But, it's really important to count the

cost of becoming a Christian. Throughout my time as a youth pastor, I've known many students who professed faith in Christ because they wanted all of his promises, but they didn't actually want to change anything about their lives. They wanted their friendships and their habits to stay the same. When the Bible sought to correct a sinful habit or character trait, they'd often say, "Nah, that's just the way I am. I thought I'm saved by faith anyway, not by works. So, what's the big deal?" The message of the gospel calls us to repentance and personal holiness. Historically, this has also included suffering and persecution because of one's identification as a Christian—and that seems increasingly common for today's teenagers. If you want to live your own version of "the good life," without God telling you what to do, then you don't want Christianity.

Dietrich Bonhoeffer was a pastor in Germany in the years before and during Hitler's reign. One of his chief concerns for German Christians was the way they identified as Christians and claimed the grace of God for themselves, but they had cheapened that grace in ways that permitted them to ignore what the Bible plainly teaches. He writes about the costly grace of the gospel this way:

> Such grace is costly because it calls us to follow, and it is grace because it calls us to follow Jesus Christ. It is costly because it costs a man his life, and it is grace because it gives a man the only true life. It is costly because it condemns sin, and it is grace because it justifies the sinner. Above all, it is costly because it cost God the life of his Son [. . .] and what has cost God much cannot be cheap for us. Above all, it is grace because God did not reckon his Son too dear a price to pay for our life, but delivered him up for us.[1]

Unfortunately, it's fairly common for teenagers to hear the promise of the gospel (Salvation! Eternal life! Adoption as a child of God!) without being told there is a cost (repentance from sin, submission to God, and oftentimes persecution). My prayer is that Bonhoeffer's words would invite you to consider the promise *and the cost* of the gospel—otherwise you may have good reasons to experience insecurity over your salvation. There is the very real possibility that you've been assured of your salvation by a well-meaning youth leader or parent, but you've never actually repented of your sin. You know there's *something* missing in your faith, but you don't know what. That missing something just might be repentance and counting the cost.

You see, the gospel is more than an invitation to find deep joy and receive eternal life some day in the future. That's why we count the cost—to be confident that we actually want to follow Jesus today, not just receive his rewards after death. None of us follow Christ perfectly. We continue to battle sin and temptation, and we often lose. But this is where we need to remember the gospel of grace: God saves sinners—and he will bring your salvation to completion! He won't abandon you during those seasons when you feel like a hypocritical or fake Christian. Those are the times when he is calling out to you with that same grace that drew you to the cross the first time. Receive God's saving grace through faith in Jesus, walk in the new life that God has in store for you, and continue to walk (and repent) by faith.

How Do I Know I'm Really a Christian?

It's common to question your salvation, especially as a teenager . . . and even more so if you're a teenager who grew up in church. If you've ever attended an evangelistic camp or retreat, you probably heard a preacher invite non-Christians to receive the gospel by praying a "sinner's prayer." It usually sounds something like, "Dear God, I confess that I am a sinner and cannot save myself. Please forgive me of my sin through Jesus Christ's death and resurrection and give me new life in him. Amen." Responding to the gospel through prayer is a good thing, obviously. But some have treated this type of prayer as a magical incantation—as if the prayer, rather than faithful repentance, is what makes someone a Christian. You may have struggled to know whether or not you're *actually* a Christian because you can't remember a time when you, well, weren't. Whether or not you're questioning your salvation because you wonder if your prayer "worked," or if it's because you don't ever remember "praying the prayer" at all, then here are some suggestions to help you find some clarity.

1. **Confess Your Sin.** The gospel is the message that God saves sinners through faith in Jesus Christ. That means you need to admit that you're a sinner, and that you cannot save yourself. Do you confess this is true about you? Read chapter one again. If you can say, "Yes, that's what I believe" then you're a Christian! And remember, Christians confess their sin with confidence that they've already been forgiven, not in order to get re-saved. If you haven't confessed your sin, then take this opportunity to prayerfully admit your sin to God—be specific and ask God to forgive you through Jesus.

2. **Confess Faith in Jesus Christ.** Salvation is the work of God. Romans 6:23 is a helpful verse to memorize: "For the wages of sin is death, but the free gift of God is eternal life in Christ Jesus our Lord." Do you trust Jesus for your salvation, rather than hoping you're good enough? Through faith in Jesus, by his virgin birth, sinless life, substitutionary death, bodily resurrection, glorious ascension, and eventual return you receive adoption as holy and deeply loved children of God. Confessing faith in Jesus Christ means you are trusting in *his* righteousness and holiness. Your salvation doesn't depend on you—it is the work of God. That's good news, because it reminds us that it isn't the strength of our faith, but the Object of our faith—Jesus Christ—that secures our relationship with God.

3. **Repent.** It's common for people to get tongue-tied over the difference between confession and repentance. Confession is "admitting the truth," while repentance means "changing your mind." For example: someone can confess that they gossip. But if they confess it, and then continue gossiping without any effort to stop, then they've simply admitted the truth about their sin without experiencing any meaningful regret about it. Repentance doesn't always mean you'll be able to perfectly stop doing what you're repenting of, but you're trying to resist temptation and to pursue God's will instead. Confession without repentance can lead us to question our salvation because we know we're not living in agreement with God's commandments.

4. **Trust God.** God's grace is eternally greater than our imperfect faith and halfhearted repentance. No one confesses or repents perfectly. Every one of us will stumble our way through conversion—and that's the beauty of it. God's perfect grace has the power to remove our guilt and shame and to give a new heart and identity to each person who believes.

5. **Seek Community.** Don't try to follow Jesus alone. Christianity is a community religion. When you become a Christian, you become part of the largest and most diverse group of people the world has ever known. So why would you even try to follow Jesus apart from others who are doing the same thing? If you're a Christian, you simply aren't meant to follow Jesus alone . . . and if you are, then that may explain why something doesn't feel right. And if you are part of a church but you're playing pretend with others, as if everything in your life is fine, then that can also contribute to your struggle. Seek genuine Christian community, where you can be honest together about the joys and the trials of following Jesus as a Christian teenager. Finding a gospel-loving church and youth group will provide meaningful support and encouragement. Trust me, you are not alone.

As you continue to follow Jesus, take comfort in knowing there are times when even your spiritual heroes struggle. If faith were easy, we'd all be a lot better at this. When faith is hard, that's when you need it most. Don't give into despair, and don't beat yourself up over the doubts you may experience. Instead, remember that your faith isn't about you—it's about God and what he's done to save you. That also means you are safely held by his hands when your faith is so small you wonder if you're a Christian at all. After all, if Christ demonstrated his love for you by dying for you while you were still his enemy, why would he give up on you now (see Romans 5:8)?

Digging Deeper

Use these questions for your own personal reflection and journaling, or for discussion with others.

- What are some reasons you think someone might be unsure whether they have genuine faith or not?
- Have you ever been invited to "count the cost" of being a Christian? What do you think that means?
- How much faith do you think is necessary before you can be sure of your salvation?
- If you're still unsure about your salvation, write a prayer below asking for God's help to find peace, and write down the name of someone who you can talk with about your uncertainty.

3
Can I Trust and Understand the Bible?

T he Bible was put together hundreds of years after Jesus lived."

"What good can a two-thousand-year-old book be for today's world?"

"That's just your interpretation."

These are statements you've likely heard or asked. I have noticed that when students fall away from faith it often begins when they stop viewing the Bible as the inspired and authoritative Word of God. Some merely look for ways to marginalize Scripture in order to live in sin. But others genuinely wrestle with the relevance and reliability of a two-thousand-year-old book.

If the Bible is just another book, then it can give advice but not make demands. The historical trustworthiness of Scripture matters because the Bible isn't an instruction manual for life, but God's revelation of himself through the person and work of Jesus Christ. Christians who lose confidence in the authority and trustworthiness of Scripture soon find themselves floundering in faith. Let's look at some reasons why you can follow Jesus with confidence in the Word of God.

ARCHAEOLOGY AFFIRMS THE BIBLE

Each book of the Bible was written with ink on a scroll and carefully recopied over the centuries. Many ancient copies have since been lost or destroyed, but what we've unearthed gives us an accurate biblical text in the original languages. When historians compare the vast number of ancient copies against other ancient texts that are highly regarded for their insight into the ancient world, and consider how few years separate those manuscripts from when the original New Testament letters were written, the historical reliability of the Bible is simply unparalleled.[1] It is unreasonable to expect that we must still have the original biblical documents in order to affirm the authenticity of the Bible. No one would make a similar demand of any other ancient document.

When compared against other ancient manuscripts, and even against the works of William Shakespeare, scholars' ability to recreate the Bible's original manuscript is unmatched. This is not a matter of opinion, but is objectively true. Plato's *Four Dialogues*, which is read in many introductory philosophy courses, has around 200 ancient copies that scholars use to piece together the original book. But when it comes to the New Testament, there are more than 5,800 copies, some of which are dated within a hundred years of the original writings. The reliability of the Old Testament was secured by the discovery of the Dead Sea Scrolls in 1946, which showed that the Hebrew text has remained the same over the last two thousand years.[2] Even atheistic archaeologists must admit the Old and New Testaments are historically reliable.

When scholars compare these ancient biblical manuscripts, the differences between texts are almost always about grammar or spellings, and none of the remaining differences affect any central doctrines.[3] This is objective, historic truth—and yet many students hear that the Bible can't be trusted. Addressing this head-on through archaeology and textual criticism assures us that the Bible we hold in our hands is a faithful translation of the original text.

HOW THE BIBLE WAS PUT TOGETHER

Sometimes people share conspiracy theories about how some books were included in the Bible while others were left out. But the Bible was not compiled by a select group of elite influencers. Leaders in the early church did not *grant* authority to certain books to become the Word of God; they affirmed which ones *already* carried authority as being "God-breathed" (2 Timothy 3:16 NIV). The identified books were then included in the canon of the New Testament.[4]

During the time of the early church, a "canon" was a rod of papyrus used as a ruler to make accurate and authoritative measurements. This terminology eventually found its way into the church's method for determining whether or not a book "measured up" and belonged within the biblical canon of Holy Scripture. The canon of the Old Testament was already established. Some new books, like the Gospel of Thomas and other Gnostic gospels, simply did not measure up to three criteria:

1. **Biblical: God's Word is consistent.** The New Testament must not contradict the Old Testament, because God does not contradict himself. The Old and New Testaments tell one consistent story of God's plan to rescue his children and reestablish his kingdom. The Gnostic gospels were dismissed from the canon because their teachings simply did not measure up with biblical teaching, especially on creation and salvation.

2. **Apostolic: Firsthand authorship.** There was early agreement that the teachings of the apostles and other firsthand witnesses of Jesus's life, death, and resurrection would be prioritized. For instance, Matthew was an apostle who was present for most of what he reported in his gospel. Paul

had a direct encounter with Jesus on the road to Damascus and received an apostolic commission. Luke got his information from firsthand sources who walked with Jesus. All the books of the New Testament were written within the lifetime of the apostles and carry the mark of apostolic teaching.

3. **Catholic: Widespread readership.** As books were considered for the canon, churches throughout the Roman Empire (and beyond) were already reading the biblical books as part of their gathered worship. This happened because of the first two criteria: Christians made copies of the Gospels and of letters that reflected gospel authority and carried these to other churches for their benefit. At the time the canon was formalized, Gospels and epistles that were only read in certain areas came up short because they demonstrated too much particularity and too little catholic (universal) appeal. The books of the New Testament were already largely accepted as authoritative by every church throughout the Christian world.

PRACTICAL IMPLICATIONS OF THE BIBLE'S RELIABILITY

- The Bible's reliability gives us confidence that the Bible we read is what the apostles actually wrote. It is common to hear that the Bible wasn't created until centuries after Jesus lived and that certain books were left out for political purposes. But archaeology demonstrates that's not true. Knowing how the Bible was actually compiled affirms our confidence in the reliability of Scripture.

- It anchors Christians within a diverse family of faith. Christianity is not a trendy religion that will be outdated by the time you graduate from high school. It is a two-thousand-year-old religion that has stood the test of time, weathered intense persecutions, and united people from every language and culture. When we read the Bible, we can be assured that God's truth is both timeless and relevant to transform our own lives today.

- Jesus really lived, died, and rose from the grave. Christianity is not just a good idea; it is a historically driven religion. The archaeological reliability of the Bible bolsters our faith in the truth of the gospel. This is especially important when our faith begins to waver. That's when we need to be anchored in the truth that the Bible is not merely spiritually true but also historically true.

Digging Deeper

Use these questions for your own personal reflection and journaling, or for discussion with others.

- What are some reasons people question the trustworthiness of the Bible?
- What did you learn about biblical archaeology? How does this affect your view of the Bible's reliability?
- How would you summarize the way the early Church discerned which books to include in the Bible?
- What do we lose when we lose the trustworthiness of Scripture? How would that affect the way you think about God, yourself, and life?

4
What Is the Trinity?

The youth group was painting Alice's house as a service project. She was an older woman with a spitfire personality. She immediately clicked with a number of our students—and with me. Over the course of the following year, we had many conversations about faith and theology, but we regularly seemed to return to her questions and hesitations about the Trinity. She simply could not accept that the Father, Son, and Holy Spirit are one. Finally, I told her, "Alice, if you do not believe that God is the Trinity, then you are not a Christian."

This might seem like an overstatement, but it's not. How can anyone consider herself a Christian if she doesn't know who God is? That was the last conversation about the Trinity we had for quite a few months. One Sunday after the benediction, she approached me with a smile across her face and declared, "I get it. A friend helped me understand. Thank you for helping me see how important it is to believe God is the Trinity, three in one."

Few areas of Christian theology are more mysterious, or more important, than the Trinity. The most important differences between the Abrahamic religions—Judaism, Christianity, and Islam—can be traced back to the Trinity, for it is God the Son who came to save sinners, and the Holy Spirit who adopts and unites the Christian with God. If someone understands the Trinity, they have a basic understanding of the most important Christian teachings. The Trinity reveals to us who God is (Father, Son, Holy Spirit), what he is like (holy, eternal, sovereign), how he deals with humanity (as Creator, Savior, Advocate, Judge), and what he expects of us (to love and honor one another the way each person of the Trinity loves and honors the others). If you claim to be a Christian but don't believe in the Trinity, then you don't believe in the Jesus of the Bible whom Christians have worshipped for two millennia.

Statements like these can be difficult to swallow because we can think, *But I don't understand the Trinity. Does that mean I'm not a Christian after all?* Breathe. The Trinity is probably the most complex doctrine of Christianity to understand—one that none of us will ever fully comprehend. But we do need a basic understanding that we worship one God, in three Persons—Father, Son, and Holy Spirit. The nature of the Trinity is mysterious and beyond our full understanding. As strange as that might be, it's actually a good thing. A god whose nature easily makes sense to the human brain must be a pretty small god. God's holiness means that he is separate and different from us. But because he is not hiding himself from us, God has revealed enough of his nature to us through the Holy Scriptures for us to understand the following explanation of the Trinity.

The doctrine of the Trinity states that God exists as one God in three persons: God the Father, God the Son, and God the Spirit. Each person of the Trinity is equally and fully God, distinct from the others, and yet they remain just one God. The Bible teaches the Trinity beginning with the days of creation. It tells how God spoke, how his Word (Jesus) was the agent of creation, and how the Spirit hovered over the waters (also consider how John 1:1–18 interprets Genesis 1). Then it tells how God spoke in plural, "Let us make man in our image" (Genesis 1:26), at the creation of humanity. Later, Jesus commands his disciples to baptize new believers "in the name of the Father and of the Son and of the Holy Spirit" (Matthew 28:19). Although the word *Trinity* never appears in the Bible, the teaching that God is one in three is consistent throughout Scripture, and the New Testament is particularly clear about the divine nature of the three persons.

THREE CORE ELEMENTS OF THE TRINITY

1. **Equal.** The Father is not greater than the Son and the Spirit, nor is any person lesser than any other. God the Son's label of *Son* does not mean he is inferior to the Father but portrays his role in salvation as the one who is sent by the Father as a Son who represents his family. Similarly, the Holy Spirit is not simply an errand-runner for the Father and Son but is equal in glory and is worthy of worship. The persons were never created but are equal in eternality and honor. This perfect equality and unity are why Jesus says, "Whoever has seen me has seen the Father" (John 14:9).
2. **Distinct.** Some distinct roles of the Trinity are on display in Ephesians 1:3–14. God the Father "chose us in him before the foundation of the world" (v. 4). The Christian is "in Christ" and God the Son is the one who did the work to accomplish our salvation (vv. 5, 9). And God the Holy Spirit is the one who secures our salvation like a seal that marks a document as something authoritative and legitimate (vv. 13–14). Each person of the Trinity has a particular role, and yet they work in perfect cooperation because they are one.
3. **United.** The Father, Son, and Holy Spirit are one God. The persons of the Trinity do not act in isolation from the others, as if they "go rogue." Instead, they are united as the perfect community from whom we understand what it means to love and honor one another. In John 17:20–26, Jesus's prayer for Christian unity directly flows from his own understanding of the Trinity's communion.

BREAKING DOWN THE BAD ANALOGIES

There is no perfect analogy to help explain the Trinity. The following analogies are common ways people attempt to teach the Trinity to children. For those of us who learned these imperfect analogies, it is important to know how to correct the ways they misrepresent our triune God.

Egg. This analogy equates the Trinity with the shell, the yolk, and the egg whites all composing one egg. A variation of this uses an apple (the skin, the meat, and the seeds). But this is not like the Trinity because each individual component of the egg or apple cannot be said to be a whole egg. Besides, one usually cracks an egg and discards the shell as useless. Also, the components of an egg can be separated and are not equal in value.

Water. This analogy compares the Trinity to steam, ice, and water. The Trinity, however, is simultaneously three in one, while a molecule of H_2O must be either water, steam, or ice—not all three at the same time. Other variations of this emphasize a person's relationships—a man might be a son, a husband, and a father—to express three different types of relationships flowing from the same person. This analogy reflects one of the oldest heresies: that God the Father turned into God the Son, who later turned into the Holy Spirit. God is a unity of three persons, not one person with three expressions.

Shamrock. Saint Patrick is the famous originator of this analogy. He used the three leaves of the shamrock to point to the three persons of the Trinity, but this also falls short for the same reason as the egg and apple: each leaf is a component of a shamrock, not fully a shamrock.

The following diagram, dating from the Middle Ages, is a simple (and easy to draw) way to explain the Trinity. It highlights that the three persons of the Trinity are equal and united within the godhead, yet remain distinct from one another.

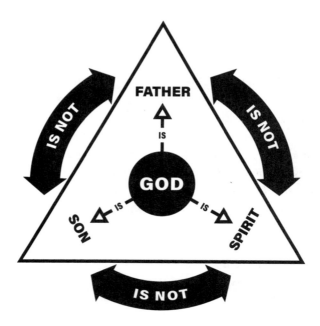

DIGGING DEEPER

Use these questions for your own personal reflection and journaling, or for discussion with others.

- If believing in the Trinity is necessary to be a Christian, why do you think we talk about it so infrequently?
- How does "equal, distinct, united" help you make sense of the relationships between the Father, Son, and Holy Spirit?
- Did you hear these or other analogies of the Trinity when you were growing up? Discuss these and other illustrations you may have heard, and highlight where the analogies are helpful and where they break down.
- Practice drawing the "shield of the trinity" diagram in the space below, explaining each part along the way.

5

Is It Okay to Doubt?

I t's common for teenagers who grew up in church to wrestle with doubt. If that describes you, then be assured that faith is a wonderful and mysterious thing, but asking hard questions is a normal part of spiritual development. Many "church kids" experience a strange combination of faith and doubt without knowing how to make sense of it. Maybe you feel plagued by difficult questions:

- What if we did "just happen" and evolved from primordial ooze?
- What if Jesus didn't really say or do the things the Bible says he did?
- How do I know God is even real?
- Why would God allow my parents to get divorced?

Many who grow up in the church feel pressure to keep their questions to themselves. Or if they do ask hard questions, they feel looked down on and are told to have more faith. I hope that's not your experience! Without the freedom to explore these doubts, many people walk away from the church—and eventually from faith. But it doesn't have to be this way.

One of my favorite stories in the Gospels comes when Jesus interacts with a man whose son is demon-possessed. When Jesus asks the man if he believes Jesus can heal the sick child, the man replies, "I believe; help my unbelief!" (Mark 9:24). We need to encourage this kind of honesty in the church.

HONEST THOMAS

One of my favorite people in the Bible is the apostle Thomas. He's usually called "Doubting Thomas," but I like to call him "Honest Thomas." After Lazarus—one of Jesus's friends and supporters—has died, Jesus wants to go to Jerusalem, even though he and the disciples have already faced opposition and threats from the religious leaders in that area. While the other disciples "remind" Jesus about the potential danger of heading to Jerusalem, Thomas dramatically says, "Let us also go, that we may die with him" (John 11:16). Can't you hear the sarcasm and sassiness in that statement? He's the type of disciple who says what everyone else is thinking. Later, after the resurrection, Thomas isn't in the room the first time Jesus appears to the other disciples. After hearing what has happened, he replies, "Unless I see the nail marks in his hands and put my finger where the nails were, and put my hand into his side, I will not believe" (John 20:25 NIV). Meanwhile, one of the verses people tend to overlook describes the disciples' attitudes when they see Jesus before he gives the Great Commission: "And when they saw him, they worshipped him, but some doubted" (Matthew 28:17). Thomas isn't the only disciple to doubt the resurrection. After all, dead people don't rise from the grave! But Jesus is patient with him and approaches Thomas, saying, "Put your finger here; see my hands. Reach out your hand and put it into my side. Stop doubting and believe" (John 20:27 NIV). There is no rebuke or frustration—only patience and mercy.

Maybe you're feeling like a Thomas in the midst of a group who has already seen the risen Christ. They're talking about how great Jesus is, and you're sitting there questioning whether or not you believe any of this could possibly be true. If this describes you, then I hope you find comfort in Thomas's example and in the way Jesus patiently and gently deals with Thomas's doubts.

BELIEVING DOUBT AND UNBELIEVING DOUBT

When you are facing doubt, please remember you don't need to doubt everything in order to doubt anything. For instance, it is entirely possible to doubt the virgin birth while still believing that God exists. Questioning one area of faith doesn't require skepticism everywhere.

I believe more youth groups need to talk about what it means to doubt from faith. This is a funny-sounding concept, but it echoes "I believe; help my unbelief." It means we stand upon those beliefs we are already convinced of, and from that platform of faith we lean into our doubts and questions. In his book, *Help My Unbelief*, Barnabas Piper talks about two kinds of doubt: "unbelieving doubt" and "believing doubt."[1] Unbelieving doubt is the kind that flows from skepticism and a lack of faith in God. On the other hand, believing doubt is what takes place when Christians express their doubts and questions while asking from a place of ongoing faith. I think this distinction is really helpful because we can easily feel like all doubt is bad. But that's just not the case. Many Christians have found their faith solidified through this kind of honest questioning.

As surprising as it may be, doubt always comes from a place of faith. Atheists doubt God's existence based on their faith in science. Universalists doubt God will judge unbelievers because of their faith in God's love and humanity's goodness. We all stand upon a set of convictions about the way things should be, and these shape the way we evaluate our doubts. Since our faith and doubts are always shaped by these core beliefs about what is good and true and beautiful, let's be aware of what those beliefs are instead of being influenced by them without realizing it.

Building on what we discussed in the previous chapter, what you believe about the Bible shapes the way you'll approach doubt. If your family and church are places where the gospel is known and loved while also being a safe place to wrestle with doubt, be very thankful. Saving faith doesn't require perfect faith. Imperfect faith (even the size of a mustard seed) that is placed in Jesus Christ is able to save because it is not about the quality of our faith, but the God in whom we have placed it.

FACING YOUR DOUBT

- **Identify wise and trustworthy guides.** You aren't the first person to ask these questions. That means you don't need to figure out all the answers on your own! Learn from others who have probably wrestled with similar questions for years.
- **Buy a journal and write about your questions.** I know you'll be tempted to open a notes app on your phone. Don't. Use pen and paper to slow your mind down, minimize distractions, and to really be deliberate about figuring out what's at the root of your doubts.
- **Practice patience.** If we want people to take our hard questions seriously, that means we shouldn't always expect our questions to be resolved quickly. Be patient as you and your trusted counselors navigate the many conversations necessary for untangling your doubt.
- **Do your homework.** Sometimes people ask hard questions and expect deep answers without needing to do any work themselves. But that's not how wisdom is ever attained. If you really want to follow your doubt to see where it leads, you may need to read some books and do some research. Ask your parent, pastor, or youth leader for trustworthy resources and books.
- **Remember that the head and heart are connected.** Even highly intellectual questions are rooted in the heart.

Consider the question, "How can a good God allow people to suffer?" That's a genuine question, but it's not a purely intellectual question—it's also a deeply personal one. As you journal about your doubts, honestly consider the ways your life experiences and emotions are shaping your intellectual questions. If you overlook this connection, even if you discover all the "right" answers, they'll be unsatisfying because it was never a purely intellectual question in the first place.

- **Keep the main thing the main thing.** There are many areas of life and faith where we can doubt—but Christianity ultimately comes down to the resurrection of Jesus Christ. If he did historically rise from the grave, then shouldn't we give his teachings greater authority?

DIGGING DEEPER

Use these questions for your own personal reflection and journaling, or for discussion with others.

- What are some reasons people are hesitant to share their doubts with one another?
- What's the difference between "believing doubt" and "unbelieving doubt?"
- Very few doubts are purely intellectual doubts. What are some ways you can see them flowing from both your head and your heart?
- What would change for you if you really trusted that Jesus's response to doubters is one of grace and patience?

6

How Can a Loving God Send Anyone to Hell?

Tolerance has so dominated our culture that it's difficult for us to reconcile the love of God with his wrath. As intimidating as it is to discuss hell and eternal judgment, it's a significant opportunity to wrestle with some of the most difficult teachings of Scripture. The Bible's teaching on hell is not a message of God's hatred for sinners, but a display of his holiness in correcting injustice and evil. It's also important to recognize the emotional weight of this conversation. Most of us are usually thinking about our non-Christian friends and family members while discussing this question. Overlooking the emotional element will lead to either a fake or guarded conversation, or a very insensitive one that leads to lots of hurt.

The gospel proclaims the grace of God in all things—even judgment and wrath. Previous generations may have heard "turn or burn" evangelistic messages at youth camps, which has led to a generation of parents and youth workers who rarely warn students about the very real judgment the Bible portrays. It is common to hear Christians admit they believe in hell because the Bible teaches about it, but admit they don't like it and wish it didn't exist. This type of thinking suggests we believe ourselves to be better judges than God—but we simply don't have the power to correct him. Such thinking shows we have a weak understanding of why hell and final judgment exist. It's important for us to understand what the Bible teaches about our loving God's judgment in both salvation and damnation.

THE BIBLE'S TEACHING ABOUT JUDGMENT AND HELL

God is perfectly holy (Exodus 3:4–6; 1 John 1:5). This means God is categorically different from and more glorious than created things. He is also the Creator (Genesis 1; Psalm 65). Therefore, all judgment belongs to God. People are not free to instruct God about the moral laws of the universe. This is clearly taught throughout Scripture (Job 38–41; Jeremiah 18:1–10). Jesus teaches that there will be a day of judgment for the righteous and the unrighteous (Matthew 25:31–46; Luke 16:19–31). This judgment will be eternal and real, reserved for both angels and humans who have sinned against God's perfect holiness (Revelation 20).

Although people often say that hell is eternal separation from God, this is not true. God's anger and judgment against sin is currently being restrained by his common grace toward all people. But there will be a day of judgment, and hell is the experience of God's unrestrained response to sin (Psalm 139:8; Romans 14:10–12). Jesus frequently taught about hell and the judgment of God, usually in parables. Based upon Jesus's own teachings, we know that hell will be eternal (Luke 16:26) and conscious (Matthew 13:42). Denying the existence of hell requires a denial of the very words of Jesus.

Two key teachings stand out as essential when we think about hell and judgment. First, sin is human rebellion against the holy God. The Bible talks about sins and transgressions. *Sin* is an archery term that means "to miss the mark" and reflects failure to meet God's holy standard of righteousness (Romans 3:23). *Transgression* means a willful breaking of God's laws (Romans 4:15). We can sin by accident or by merely falling short of keeping God's commandments perfectly, but transgression is when we knowingly choose to sin. If we're honest, every single one of us can confess being guilty of both. This is no small guilt; our sin uncovers our desire to sit on God's throne as the one who determines right and wrong in our own lives. We all want to live our own truth, even if God says something different.

Second, wrath is God's holy response to sin. Think about it: how should God respond to sinful rebels who have brought so much death and destruction into his good creation? Unlike human wrath, God's is never unfair, uncontrolled, or directed against someone who's innocent. It is not in opposition to his holiness or his love. Instead, it's a direct expression of his holy love against the injustices that sinful men and women have introduced in this world. God's wrath and judgment are the purifying fire that fertilizes the garden of Eden to be reborn in the new heaven and the new earth (Revelation 20–22). If God did not judge sin, injustice would continue, and the curse of sin (death) would never end.

Survivors of injustice and abuse understand that judgment and punishment are right and loving responses to the evil that has been perpetrated against them. They cry out for justice. And when their oppressors find ways to "work the system" and get away without any punishment, we call it injustice. In cases like this, what are we supposed to do? How are we supposed to feel? It's easy to think the entire world is unjust and corrupted—and it is! But there will be a day when all the evil and corruption will be laid bare before God and he will issue his judgment. Injustice will be revealed for what it is. Every sin will be brought into the light, and every sinner will give an account for what they have done. This isn't because God is really angry, but because his holy love is determined to restore all creation in perfect peace and harmony.

WHY HELL IS AN ESSENTIAL ELEMENT OF CHRISTIAN FAITH

The gospel is the good news that God saves sinners by faith through the grace of Jesus Christ. This means there is something we need to be saved from. If there is no judgment for sin, then there is no need for salvation. Even further, Jesus's suffering and death on a cross would be a foolish sacrifice, since we were never in danger to begin with.

Some might wonder why God cannot simply forgive sin without any judgment. After all, can't God do what he wants? The following three points are not exhaustive, but provide a basic framework to help you understand why hell and the final judgment are essential Christian doctrines.

1. **The nature of sin: rebellion against the holy God.** Most of us have heard people defend their perceived self-righteousness by saying, "I haven't killed anyone and I've never been arrested. Sure, I'm not perfect. But I'm a good person." This objection, however, misunderstands how sin is measured. The penalty of sin is not determined merely by each sin's results, but by the one against whom the sin is committed. We don't measure sin against one another's sinfulness, but against the holiness of God. All sin receives an eternal judgment because it is committed against the holy and eternal God (in addition to the people who were sinned against). My friend Kevin Yi helps his students understand the weightiness of their sin this way: consider the difference between drawing a mustache on a poster at your local grocery store (which would be wrong, but hardly something to be arrested over) and drawing a mustache on the *Mona Lisa*. You did the same thing in each instance, but who or what you do it against makes all the difference. In the same way, even our "little sins" against a holy God have rightfully earned his eternal wrath.[1] And sin is not

just individual wrong acts—it's turning away from God
and going our own way, wanting to be god of our own life.
Isaiah described the human condition like this: "all we like
sheep have gone astray; we have turned—every one—to
his own way" (Isaiah 53:6). Our actions are wrong because
our direction is wrong. God would not be holy if he simply
overlooked sin.

2.   **The character of God: the Judge.** The Bible connects God's
work of creation with his right to judge: "But who are you,
O man, to answer back to God? Will what is molded say to
its molder, 'Why have you made me like this?'" (Romans
9:20). This right to judge is because "all things were created
through him and for him" (Colossians 1:16). Quoting Scripture in response to these types of questions is not avoiding
their complexity, but recognizing there is an element of
faith involved. If you believe the Bible truly reveals to us
who God is and what he is like, then it is necessary to recognize God's judgment of sin and evil. A judge who does
not uphold the law would be considered unjust and should
be removed. Judgment is God's proper response to sin—because sin always brings death and destruction. And if you
don't believe the Bible, then of course you'll reject the neces-
sity of faith in Jesus to be saved from judgment.

3.   **The answer to the problem of evil: justice satisfied.** Anyone
who asks, "Does God care about suffering in this world?"
should find comfort in the final judgment and reality of
hell. God cares so much about justice that he will indeed
avenge those who have been wronged, oppressed, and vic-
timized. Those who live in relative comfort may struggle
with this seemingly harsh reality, but cultures where sys-
temic oppression runs rampant will frequently cry out for
judgment against those who harm them—and this is not
wrong. The cries of the martyrs in Revelation 6:10 plead for
the Lord's justice against their murderers. In fact, one reason why injustice continues in the world is God's patience in

executing judgment. The Lord's gracious patience continues to invite sinners to repent and receive grace before the day of judgment comes. In this way, hell and judgment provide a surprising resolution to one of the most common reasons people lose faith. The return of Jesus Christ will bring sin and suffering to an end because his judgment against the devil and all his works will be final, and his people will experience the fulfillment of every divine promise.

DIGGING DEEPER

Use these questions for your own personal reflection and journaling, or for discussion with others.

- Why do you think hell is an embarrassing doctrine for many Christians to talk about?
- How does the metaphor about the Mona Lisa help you understand the nature of sin and why God cannot simply overlook it?
- How does God's judgment show his love and compassion for those who have suffered injustice?
- Skeptics of the idea of hell call for a God of love and mercy, and we have one! How is the gospel evidence that God takes both sin and mercy seriously?

7
Why Did Jesus Need to Die?

C hristianity does not merely attempt to give individuals inner peace or happiness. It declares from the rooftop that God is for us, and "if God is for us, who can be against us?" (Romans 8:31). This isn't some trite wish-dream, but is anchored firmly in the cross. The death and resurrection of Jesus Christ is at the very heart of Christianity. Theologians use the funny-sounding term *penal substitutionary atonement* to describe why the cross is good news.

A DISPLAY OF GOD'S JUSTICE AND GRACE

Penal is a strange word that has to do with the court of law. It's where we get the common word *penalty*—the negative consequence someone receives after breaking a rule. As Hebrews 9:22 says, "the law requires that nearly everything be cleansed with blood, and without the shedding of blood there is no forgiveness." (NIV) By referring to Jesus's work on the cross as penal substitutionary atonement, we are recognizing that an offense has been committed that requires a penalty.

The last chapter highlighted the reasons why God's judgment on sin is so important. What happened on the cross was a display of God's justice and his grace. It was an expression of justice because God dealt with sin head-on rather than brushing it aside. The gravity of the cross reflects the seriousness of sin, which we too easily belittle.

In God's justice we also see his perfect grace shining in full brilliance. For "while we were still sinners, Christ died for us" (Romans 5:8). Jesus did not die on the cross because God painted himself into a corner, but out of the same joyful love that propels parents to sacrifice for their children (Hebrews 12:1–2). If you ever doubt the love or grace of God, look to Jesus and behold the cross.

THE BELIEVER'S SUBSTITUTE

When Jesus hung on the cross, he was the Christian's substitute. He took the wrath of God and died so that Christians would be set free as beloved children of God. For this to happen, he met two criteria: he was human (so he could stand in our place) and he was holy (so he would be a perfect sacrifice who could cover our sin). Theologians sometimes refer to Jesus as the God-man. This isn't because Jesus is half god and half man, like Hercules. Instead, it's because Jesus is God in flesh: fully God and fully human.

Because Jesus is fully God and fully human, he is a "second Adam" who was born without a sinful nature. He had the authority to forgive sin (Matthew 9:5–8), to work miracles (Matthew 12:25–29), and to give life (Mark 5:38–42). He was the substitute for sinful believers on the cross, bearing the wrath and judgment that was ours, in order that his righteousness and holiness would become ours (Romans 5:6–8; Hebrews 2:9).

ATONEMENT

Atonement has to do with a sacrifice that satisfies a judgment or penalty against someone who is guilty. Worship and grace in the Old Testament were centered around the sacrificial system, which instructed faithful Jews to bring certain offerings, such as lambs, bulls, and goats, to the temple as a sacrifice to atone for their sins. An animal offered as an atoning sacrifice was a type of substitute for the person making the sacrifice. Blood was spilled to express the judgment and wrath that should be upon the head of the person bringing the offering but instead fell onto the sacrificial animal. While the sacrifices a priest offered needed to be repeated (to atone for the sins committed since the last offering), Jesus is both the perfect sacrifice and the Great High Priest whose sacrifice is enough to be offered once for all sin (Hebrews 10:1). In this way, the substitutionary death atoned for the sin of the worshipper.

When Jesus came onto the scene, John the Baptist called him, "the Lamb of God, who takes away the sin of the world" (John 1:29). The sacrificial system was built as a shadow of the true substitutionary sacrifice: Jesus Christ, the Lamb of God. Jesus is the sacrificial lamb whose blood was spilled to make atonement for others. Rather than offering a sacrifice that would need to be repeated, Jesus's death was sufficient to atone for the sins of all those who believe—once and for all (Hebrews 10:1–18; 1 Peter 3:18).

THE CENTRALITY OF THE CROSS

Understanding *penal substitutionary atonement* can help you understand why the cross was necessary and what God accomplished through it. The cross lies at the heart of the gospel because it is where the holy love of God is most clearly displayed. Without the cross, there are only more commandments to fulfill, and to break, and to atone for. But thanks be to Jesus, who perfectly kept the commandments and gives us his righteousness while taking away our sin.

DIGGING DEEPER

Use these questions for your own personal reflection and journaling, or for discussion with others.

- How would your faith be affected if you found out that Jesus never actually died?
- The Old Testament is marked by animal sacrifice as the pathway to forgiveness; how is that a foreshadowing of what was fulfilled through the cross?
- *Penal substitutionary atonement* is a really weird phrase, but it's an important one to understand what happened on the cross. How would you describe it to a friend?
- When Jesus died, he atoned for all sin in that moment—past, present, future. How does it strengthen you to live with greater peace and freedom to realize that even your future sins have already been atoned for and forgiven?

8

How Do We Know Jesus Rose from the Grave?

W hat would happen if we found out Jesus never rose from the grave? This is a common question. And it is a welcome one, since the gospel offers help not only in joyful seasons but also in questioning ones. How do we really know that Jesus rose from the grave? And if he didn't, how much of a difference would that make?

Paul's words in 1 Corinthians 15:17 are crucial: "If Christ has not been raised, your faith is futile and you are still in your sins." Our Christian hope is in the risen Christ, not merely in a set of philosophical truths: "He who raised Christ Jesus from the dead will also give life to your mortal bodies" (Romans 8:11). This is a hinge on which all Christianity swings. If Jesus has not risen from the grave, we are wasting our time. But if he has, that changes everything. This is the primary truth we return to over and over.

So, how can you grow in confidence that the resurrection really happened? The following proofs of the resurrection can help strengthen your confidence in the new life promised by the gospel.

Eyewitnesses. The New Testament writers claim they actually saw Jesus. This was unexpected and surprising, to the point that the disciples did not even believe it when they were first told (Luke 24:11, 38–43; John 20:19–29). Those who say the apostles stole the body of Jesus out of the tomb forget that Roman guards were stationed to seal and protect the tomb—and if they allowed bandits to raid the tomb, it would cost them their lives. The guards were indeed bribed—but not by the apostles. The bribe came from the chief priests who had the money and political authority to protect the guards in exchange for their silence. More than that, the disciples went so far as to say that Jesus's resurrection was physical and bodily, not just spiritual or metaphorical. Jesus's wounds were visible and touchable, and the closing chapters of both Luke and John contain accounts of eating with Jesus that reinforce this glorious hope (ghosts can't eat). It is also notable that the first people to see the risen Christ were women. This detail is significant because women weren't highly regarded and could not even provide legal testimony in court. If Jesus's resurrection had been a fabricated story, only a fool would make women the first witnesses. The prominence of the women in this account can only be explained by its historical accuracy.

The Date of Early New Testament Documents. Many of the original readers of the New Testament Gospels and letters were also eyewitnesses if they had traveled to Jerusalem for Passover the year Jesus rose. These eyewitnesses were still alive when the Gospels were written and could have easily refuted any reports that were made up. While writing about the truth of the resurrection, Paul writes, "He appeared to Cephas, then to the twelve. Then he appeared to more than five hundred brothers at one time, most of whom are still alive, though some have fallen asleep" (1 Corinthians 15:5–6). Paul essentially says, "If you don't believe Jesus rose from the dead, go talk to some of the other people who all saw him—they're still alive."

Non-Christian Writers. The life, death, and resurrection of Jesus Christ is mentioned by multiple non-Christian writers in the ancient world. Of course, they did not believe he actually rose from the grave, but they remarked about the apostles' claim that he did.[1] This is historic evidence that something significant happened in Jerusalem leading to a movement of people who were convinced Jesus was the Messiah who rose from the dead, ascended into heaven, and will come again as Judge and Savior.

A Drastic Change in the Disciples. The Gospels routinely share instances where Jesus corrects his disciples for having little faith. When Jesus was arrested, they all deserted him and ran for their lives. Then, suddenly, they were on the streets during the festival of Pentecost preaching the gospel and declaring the resurrection of Jesus. From that day on, they endured intense opposition and persecution without wavering. If they had agreed to lie about the resurrection, what are the chances they would all endure persecution unto death over something they knew was not true? Each of the apostles was killed for proclaiming the resurrection, except for the apostle John, who died in exile on the small island of Patmos. Surely something happened to bring about such radical change. Jesus's bodily resurrection was the historic claim that launched the worldwide church. Given all the evidence, it is entirely reasonable to place your faith in Jesus Christ as the risen Savior.

REAL-LIFE IMPACT OF THE RESURRECTION

- The resurrection proves Jesus is the Son of God. Everything he said about himself is true.
- When you doubt, the resurrection can bolster your faith. It's easy to doubt philosophical ideas like the existence of God and the Trinity. But the resurrection is an event that anchors Christianity in history. If Jesus actually rose from the grave, then you can also believe what he says about God, the Old Testament, and about life in general.

- You can live with hope even in the midst of suffering. Christians will share in Christ's victory over sin and death. No matter what's going on in and around you, there is always a reason for hope: Jesus has defeated your greatest enemy.
- When you grieve the death or sickness of a friend or family member, you will experience grief but need not grieve as those who have no hope (1 Thessalonians 4:13). Instead, you can believe the gospel's promise that death is the transition from this life into the very presence of God, where believers experience the fullness of God's blessing as we await the new heaven and new earth.

DIGGING DEEPER

Use these questions for your own personal reflection and journaling, or for discussion with others.

- How would your faith change if you found out that Jesus never rose from the grave?
- How would you summarize this chapter's claims about the importance of the resurrection?
- What stands out to you from the evidence of Jesus's resurrection?
- Why does the historic truth of the resurrection help Christians live with hope and optimism?

9

Will Jesus Really Return?

Jesus will finish what he started. There will be a day when every single promise of God will be fulfilled, and we'll see him with our own eyeballs. The return of Christ is wrapped in a fair amount of mystery, but it's not unimportant. So if Christians actually believe Jesus will return, why don't we hear more about it at church?

Pastors often give two main reasons for rarely teaching about the end times: there are so many views that it's hard to speak without feeling pressure to give every perspective equal time, and it sometimes leads to obsession among those who believe Jesus's return is only days away. This means that many of us continue to struggle with unanswered questions about Christ's return. When your earthly hopes are crushed or you find yourself in seasons of suffering, you can be reminded that God's eternal promise of glory is the best news because when Jesus returns, he will finish everything he started. It is a great comfort to remember that "the sufferings of this present time are not worth comparing with the glory that is to be revealed to us" (Romans 8:18). In the end, everything will be okay.

Why Christ's Return Is Essential

The Bible clearly teaches that Christ will come again (Acts 1:11; James 5:8, Revelation 22:20, for example). If that's not going to happen, it means Jesus's understanding of his mission was faulty and unreliable—and unfinished. Currently, salvation is secure but incomplete. Jesus has defeated sin and death, but his return to claim that victory will put an eternal end to their very existence.

Christian hope longs for the day when our faith will become sight and when all of God's promises receive their glorious fulfillment. Without the return of Jesus, Christians would continue to live in a world marred by sin, with daily temptations to break God's law. Although death's sting no longer brings an eternal death sentence, it still produces intense grief and sorrow in this life. But when Jesus ushers in the new heaven and new earth described in Revelation 21 and 22, we will experience an even greater Eden where the potential for sin will have been eliminated. In this way, the gospel is secure and fulfilled, but not yet complete. This is why his return is worthy of being shouted from the rooftops—not because it is a fear-inducing evangelism tactic, but because it fills us with confidence that God's promise of salvation outshines all of our expectations.

What All Christians Believe about Christ's Return

Despite the differences between various end-times views, there are certain truths we must affirm to keep in step with historic Christian faith. Although many of us are drawn to exploring the differences between different Christian viewpoints, it's important to highlight the shared convictions that bind Christians together as we prayerfully anticipate Christ's return.

Visibility. Acts 1:11 explicitly says, "This Jesus, who was taken up from you into heaven, will come in the same way as you saw him go into heaven." As with the resurrection, there are some who try to say Christ's return will be spiritual, not physical—but

that view has been considered outside the boundaries of faithful Christianity since the days of the apostles. The promised
new heaven and new earth will be real (not just spiritual), just as
Jesus's return will be real and visible for all to behold.

Judgment. Jesus will return as the Judge. All the sin and
evil and injustice that has been perpetrated on earth will receive
its rightful judgment. Those who question, "Why doesn't God
stop all this suffering and evil?" will discover that he was not
turning a blind eye after all, but patiently giving sinners time
to repent. All who have placed their faith in Jesus Christ for
salvation will be declared innocent children of God who receive
eternal life. Those not in Christ will receive eternal damnation
as sinners who have rebelled against the holy God (Revelation
20:11–15). Christians do not to teach this in order to scare people
into faith, but to warn them about the terrible consequences of
sin and to display for them the fullness and glory of our salvation through Christ.

Salvation. Teaching about judgment and salvation go hand
in hand. Without hearing about sin and judgment, there is no
need for salvation in the first place. The gospel proclaims God's
victory over sin and death through the cross and empty tomb.
We will leap with joy over the fulfillment of every gospel promise in the new heaven and new earth.

Kingdom. Even if you grew up in church, you might be
astounded to hear that we will have real, physical bodies in the
new heaven and new earth. This isn't something we talk about
often enough. The kingdom of God is usually taught in ways
that are so abstract and spiritual there is no real consideration
for the biblical language of Isaiah 65 and Revelation 21, which
describe a renewed earth that is also the heavenly place of God,
since he has come to live with his people. When Jesus returns
as Savior and Judge, all creation will rejoice in salvation's fulfillment. Sin and death will have no place, for the kingdom of
God will be fully realized and God's children will enjoy it for all
eternity. This is good news indeed.

MAKING SENSE OF THE DIFFERENT END-TIMES VIEWS

Details surrounding the end times, like the rapture (a sudden removal of all Christians prior to the great persecution known as the tribulation), millennium (the literal one-thousand-year reign of Jesus as king of the earth), and role of Israel (will it be restored as the primary residence of Christ during the millennium?), are hotly contested issues that sometimes cause division between Christians when we lose sight of the clear truths we agree on. The following is a brief summary of the four major views on end times (or "eschatology," if we want to get technical) that fall within the realm of evangelical Christianity. It is helpful to have a basic understanding of these views in order to appreciate other Christians who believe differently than you, since there is not one definitive view that every Christian must have about the end times in order to have genuine faith.

Dispensational premillennialism. In the dispensational view, salvation history is broken into eras (long periods of time, known as dispensations) in which God deals with his people in different ways. We are currently living in the sixth of seven dispensations, with the millennial kingdom yet to come. Dispensationalists believe Jesus's return will be a two-stage event: first he will return to rapture Christians (both living and dead) out of the world as a rescue from the great tribulation (a period of significant persecution and suffering), and then he will return after a seven-year tribulation to usher in the millennial (thousand-year) kingdom. The final judgment takes place upon Jesus's full return, after the tribulation (where there will be significant persecution and suffering), and will introduce the new heaven and new earth. While this view has become prevalent among Christians in North America in the past two hundred years, historic premillennialism is the most historically-attested premillennial view.

Historic premillennialism. According to historic premillennialism, Jesus will return after the great tribulation to establish the millennial kingdom on earth. Most historic premillenialists do not believe in a two-stage rapture of the church (like dispensationalists do), but that believers will be raptured to meet with Christ in the clouds in order to greet him and usher him into his millennial kingdom. At that time, there will be a great influx of Jewish believers, and Christians will reign with Christ over the nations for one thousand years. Sin will remain, but will be kept in check by the rule of Christ. At the end of the millennium there will be a great judgment of Satan and of all those who oppose Christ, and the eternal kingdom of God will be fully established in the new heaven and new earth.

Amillennialism. This position states that the millennium is not a literal thousand years but a symbolic duration of time that began with Christ's resurrection, or at Pentecost, and will continue until Christ's return. In this view, the tribulation and millennium happen simultaneously: Christians today are actively persecuted even as the church expands throughout the whole earth through the proclamation of the gospel. Amillennialists do not believe the Bible teaches anything about a rapture of Christians out from persecution, but that God strengthens his people to endure opposition. The final judgment will take place immediately when Jesus returns, at which time he will usher in the new heaven and new earth.

Postmillennialism. In this view, the tribulation has already taken place and the church is presently ushering in the millennium through the spread of the gospel. Sin will not cease, but it will be greatly minimized as the gospel transforms cultures. When the nations have been evangelized and the influence of the gospel has reached its peak, Jesus will return and establish the new heaven and new earth.

DIGGING DEEPER

Use these questions for your own personal reflection and journaling, or for discussion with others.

- Do conversations about the end times fill you with hope or fear? Why?
- What are some beliefs about the end times that all Christians agree on? Put them in your own words.
- This chapter claims, "the gospel is secure and fulfilled, but not yet complete." What does this mean and how is it connected to the end times?
- Read Revelation 21–22. How do these chapters give you a clearer picture of what awaits Christians in glory?

10
Who (Not What) Is the Holy Spirit?

The Holy Spirit is the third person of the Trinity, equal with the Father and the Son. This is why it is concerning when Christians call the Holy Spirit an "it" rather than "he." Personal pronouns exist to highlight personal agency. We need God's personal presence, not an impersonal force.

Many Christians feel intimidated when talking about the Holy Spirit. The Father and the Son (Jesus) are easy to discuss, but discussing the Holy Spirit seems mystical and unfamiliar. Additionally, the gifts of the Spirit are controversial, so it feels safer to leave the Holy Spirit to professional theologians. And yet, the Holy Spirit is God. Maturing as a disciple involves developing a clear view of the Holy Spirit, who equips us to walk in step with the Spirit and to rely on his strength for our sanctification. If Christians avoid talking about the Holy Spirit, they will have an unbiblical understanding of the God they claim to worship.

WHAT THE HOLY SPIRIT DOES

- **Applies salvation to the believer.** All three persons of the Trinity are involved in the work of salvation. The Father sent the Son to make atonement for sinners, and the Spirit applies that gift of grace to the children of God. He brings conviction of sin that leads sinners to saving faith in Christ (John 16:8) and unites them to Christ (1 John 4:13). He clothes us in the righteousness of Christ and does the inner work of sanctification (2 Thessalonians 2:13).

- **Advocates.** The Holy Spirit is sometimes called the *Paraclete*, which comes from the Greek word used in John's gospel that's translated as "Helper," "Advocate," or "Counselor" (John 14:15–17). The Bible describes the Spirit's ministry not primarily as that of a counselor–therapist (giving us advice when we ask), but a counselor–lawyer (advocating for us before the judge). He even prays for us when we don't know what to say (Romans 8:26–27).

- **Teaches.** The Holy Spirit not only speaks to the Father on our behalf, but also gives us the words to speak to others. Mark 13:11 has a helpful explanation: "And when they bring you to trial and deliver you over, do not be anxious beforehand what you are to say, but say whatever is given you in that hour, for it is not you who speak, but the Holy Spirit." The Spirit is the teacher of God's people. Jesus promised that when he went away, "the Helper, the Holy Spirit, whom the Father will send in my name, he will teach you all things and bring to your remembrance all that I have said to you" (John 14:26). This promise was given directly to the apostles who would carry the gospel into the world. It continues to remind Christians of the Holy Spirit's ongoing help today, as he illuminates our minds to the Word of God in Scripture. This promise also bolsters our confidence in the Scriptures as being "breathed out by God" (2 Timothy 3:16) because the authors were under the guidance of the Holy Spirit. The Christian's confidence in sharing the gospel with his or her friends is strengthened by Jesus's promise in Acts 1:8 that the Holy Spirit empowers the work of the Great Commission. This Spirit-wrought confidence is displayed in Acts 4:31.

- **Sanctifies.** Christians are being transformed into the image of Christ (Romans 15:16; Colossians 3:10). This is the sanctifying work of the Holy Spirit who unites us with Christ by faith (1 Corinthians 3:16). The Spirit applies the grace of God, leads sinners to repentance, and strengthens believers in the midst of temptation—even in ways they are likely unaware of. We read of "the fruit of the Spirit," not the fruit of our efforts, because godliness is the result of the Spirit's work rather than the Christian's hard work to produce it (Galatians 5:22). Although parents and youth workers may play a pivotal role in your spiritual growth, it is the Holy Spirit who will ultimately convict your heart, transform your life, and apply the righteousness of Christ to you.

- **Gives gifts.** The Holy Spirit empowers God's people for ministry. The Bible's lists of spiritual gifts do not create a hierarchy of important people in the church; they show that all believers with all kinds of gifts contribute to building up the church. This should empower Christians to live in a way that each of us (regardless of age) plays an important role in Christ-exalting ministry among God's people and among the spiritually lost. Teenage Christians are genuine members of Christ's Church with gifts that are intended to build up the body of Christ and to extend ministry in the community. God equips those he calls, often while they are in the midst of obedience rather than before. For this reason, dear reader, if you're a Christian, please consider the way you are trusting God to use you to exalt the name of Jesus.

WALKING IN STEP WITH THE SPIRIT

All Christians, regardless of their age, are called to walk in step with the Spirit (Galatians 5:16–26). This involves turning away from sin and walking in Spirit-prompted holiness. We will not grow if we stand still or avoid the Spirit. But we joyfully remember that the gospel is not a message that cries out "try harder, do better." It is an invitation to cease striving and to take a walk with God throughout your day.

In a culture that places great emphasis on dreaming big and changing the world (consider the most popular themes of high school commencement speeches), the gospel invites us to rest in Christ and walk with him. The following habits are not presented as a to-do list, but simply as practices that are common among us when we are walking in step with the Spirit.

First, we trust the Word of God. How can we trust God's Word if we do not read it? Learning how to read and apply the Bible as a lifelong practice may be the single most effective thing we can do as young Christians. We call the Bible the "Word of God" for a reason: God continues to speak through it. Are we listening? When we walk in the Spirit, we walk with the Bible in our hands.

Second, we have a deepening prayer life. We not only pray before meals or a big test, but throughout the day and during dedicated moments of intercession for others. When we are growing in the faith, we will experience a deepening fellowship with God, and this happens largely through prayer. See chapter 19 for more on the importance of prayer.

Third, we want to see the gospel transform others' lives. Walking in step with the Spirit doesn't guarantee a spiritual high or warm fuzzies. But if we are drawing near to God, then we will be more likely to talk about him with others. When we have experienced the new life that comes by faith in Jesus, then we want others to experience it too. Not everyone is a natural or passionate evangelist—and that's okay. This is not a mysterious spiritual gift only a few receive, but a basic Christian conviction: "This is the greatest message in the world, I want to share it with others, as the Lord provides opportunities." Do we pray for opportunities to talk about Jesus with others?

Fourth, we want to be with the people of God. Being at church and youth group will not be measured by how entertaining and fun it is, but will become a sweet experience because there is a growing sense of, "These are my people. I belong here." Do we believe that we are members of the family of God, or do we only want to participate in youth group activities that are fun?

Fifth, we will humbly receive correction from parents, youth workers, and other authority figures. If we cannot receive correction from human authority figures, we are more likely to resist correction from God. Living with a teachable and correctable spirit doesn't make us weak or insecure. It simply means we're humble enough to know we are sinners who have more to learn.

Finally, we take risks. No, I'm not talking about cliff jumping or driving without a seat belt. Walking by faith means we actually trust God. And if we trust God, then we'll find ourselves in situations that we cannot control and where we don't know how things will turn out. Talking about faith with non-Christian peers, forgiving someone who's been a bully, and speaking up for those who are vulnerable can be a really scary thing. If we always do things we can control, then there's no need to walk by faith—because we aren't relying on the Spirit's power or provision.

In all these ways, walking by faith will make us different from our non-Christian peers. We will live with an abiding awareness that we are dependent on the strength of the Holy Spirit. Walking in step with the Spirit is not for superpowered Christians, but for everyone—teenagers included—whose lives demonstrate the faithfulness of God to save sinners like us.

DIGGING DEEPER

Use these questions for your own personal reflection and journaling, or for discussion with others.

- Do you think about the Holy Spirit as being equal with God the Father and with Jesus, or as less important? Why?

- Why is it essential for us to call the Holy Spirit "him," not "it"?
- How does the section on "Walking in Step with the Spirit" help you better understand the ministry of the Holy Spirit?
- What's going on in your life right now where you could use the Holy Spirit's help to walk by faith?

11
Why Is the Church Important?

C hurch doesn't seem like something that still holds relevance for many teenagers. Why go somewhere to sing boring songs, listen to a lecture, and be surrounded by a bunch of old people who don't talk to you?

But what if that's not the way it needs to be? What if those things that seem boring and outdated are actually meaningful expressions of your Christian identity?

It's common to hear people throw around statistics about the church dropout rate: two-thirds of teenagers who were active in youth ministry stop attending church between the ages of 18–22.[1] These types of surveys can be helpful, but also misleading.

Many of these surveys would consider you a "church dropout" if you're reading this book because you came to a retreat and the youth pastor gave you this book, but you only visited youth group a few times and never professed to be a Christian. Although the helpfulness of these types of studies can be debated, one of the common traits in students who remain connected to the church throughout adolescence and into adulthood is a sense of belonging in their local church. To these students, church is not simply where youth group takes place; it is a family of faith where they belong.

CHURCH KIDS WHO DON'T ACTUALLY GO TO CHURCH

I strongly believe that teenagers should be part of the church's corporate worship service. Separating them into a youth service during the corporate service might sound like a more relevant option, but it's shortsighted and only yields short-term fruit. The biblical words *church* and *synagogue* mean "gathering" or "assembly." If you are not worshipping with the gathered body of believers, then you might attend youth group or Sunday school but you do not attend church. I've seen this happen many times: church kids grow up in the children's ministry, then they attend youth group, only to eventually find their way to a college or young adults Bible study . . . then they struggle to ever feel "at home" in church. They always attended programs that were specifically geared for their age group.

Worshipping with your church means that sometimes the songs will be the types of songs other people like, and sometimes they'll be the songs that you like. Being part of a church where ten-year-olds and ninety-year-olds worship together is a beautiful but difficult thing. It means the generations will need to practice humility in order to celebrate others' preferences. This is even more true when there are different cultures and ethnicities in the church! In that case, not only are there generational preferences, but also cultural preferences about how people enjoy expressing faithful worship. But when we're able to honor these preferences, it's one of the most incredible and beautiful expressions of unity our world can witness. Despite everything else that can keep us apart, we've chosen to worship with humility in order to worship together—because we are equal members of the family of God!

WHY YOUTH GROUP ISN'T CHURCH

Going to youth group is great—but youth group is not church. The New Testament provides guidance around what a church is and how it should operate. More specifically, a church should be led by pastors, elders, and deacons (1 Timothy 3:1–13; Titus 1:5–9) and it should be devoted to worship and proclaiming the Word of God (Colossians 3:16–17), and to observing the ordinances of baptism and the Lord's Supper (Matthew 28:19–20; 1 Corinthians 12:25). Obviously, different branches of Christianity express these biblical guidelines differently, but the point remains that a youth group doesn't meet the biblical qualifications for being a church. Youth group is one single generation meeting together for a specific purpose (to make disciples of teenagers). The church is a multigenerational gathering that is led by mature Christians who have been set apart for spiritual leadership and teaching in order to lead God's people in the ordinances (baptism and communion), corporate worship (singing and preaching of God's Word), and to govern in discipleship and church discipline.

The youth ministry is the church's way to come alongside parents to pass the faith from generation to generation. If teenagers attend youth group or Sunday school but not corporate worship, they may go to the church building on Sundays, but they do not "go to church." When the generations are isolated from each other in church, it should not be surprising when students graduate and never make church a priority in their lives. Teenagers belong in the church, not just in the youth ministry, because they are not merely children in the church, but spiritual brothers and sisters in the faith with genuine value and contributions. The major exception to this is found in ethnic churches where significant cultural barriers (especially language) make it nearly impossible for the generations to worship together.

WHY TEENAGERS BELONG IN THE CHURCH

Christian teenagers, you are members of the Church. You are not junior Christians or Christians-in-training. Anyone who turns from sin and confesses faith in Jesus Christ receives the Holy Spirit and is united with Christ. This makes them members of the body of Christ, the *universal Church* (Ephesians 1:22–23). So, if you are a Christian (regardless of age), then you are a member of the universal Church and have been spiritually adopted into a family of faith that includes Christians from all languages, ethnicities, and periods of history.

For example, Christian teenagers in rural Texas are one in Christ with persecuted Christians in Iran. This means Christians are members of the most diverse, multiethnic, and persecuted group of people in the world today. The implications of these truths are enormous, including how we spend our money, intercede for others in prayer, combat racism, and think about global politics.

The *local church* is a particular expression of the universal Church. It is an organized group of Christians who have committed to gather to worship the triune God, to grow as disciples, and to proclaim the gospel to the lost. It would have been unthinkable for first-century Christians to have the freedom Western teenagers enjoy, to prefer worshipping privately at home rather than with the body of Christ.

Gathering with God's people for worship, prayer, and to hear the Scriptures preached are all God-given ways for God to shape our minds and hearts. As a longtime youth pastor, I've had many former students return to tell me how God was at work in them through the normal routine of what we do on Sunday mornings, even though they didn't realize it at the time. Worship and the faithful preaching of God's Word provided comfort and strength when their life plans crumbled. Often, the songs they sang and the Bible verses they learned while growing are how the Lord applies the gospel to their hearts and leads them into sincere and vibrant faith. Think about it this way: while so much about modern life wears out or becomes irrelevant after just a few years, the message and traditions of the Church have endured centuries of opposition.

Growing in holiness doesn't happen in solitary confinement. The first thing God said was not good was for Adam to be alone, because people were created for community. Spiritual maturity is rarely found in isolated Christians, but is found in increasing measure among those who provide fellowship and support for others. You can receive mentoring and find godly role models when you get to know other adults in the church—but this will be impossible if you are not meaningfully engaged in the life of the church and are only with your peers. You'll also learn from faithful Christians who are single, divorced, widowed, facing chronic or terminal illness, or are from a different culture or ethnicity from your own. Being part of the church gives you a window into the wide diversity of Christian godliness in ways that only being with fellow teenagers could never provide.

Ministry to others is another significant component of every Christian's spiritual development. Attending programs without any meaningful involvement turns you into a spiritual consumer who stands on the sidelines and evaluates whether or not the program is meeting your needs. That's just not what the church is supposed to be like! Pastors are called to "equip the saints for the work of ministry" (Ephesians 4:12). This includes teenagers! Sometimes teenagers can feel like there's no space for them to make a meaningful contribution in the church, while some adults assume that the next generation won't step up and only wants to play on their phones. When the generations believe the best about each other (rather than giving into negative assumptions) really incredible things can happen.

Practical Ways to Experience "Belonging" at Church

- Worship together with all generations as often as reasonably possible. If your youth group meets during the gathered worship service of the church, talk with your parents and youth leaders about why you'd like to start attending worship.
- Serve in the children's ministry. This is often the most accessible place for teenagers to begin serving, and being paired with a lead teacher provides you with a mentor.
- Get involved in existing ministries like the worship team, media ministry, or hospitality. You have gifts and passions that enable you to offer meaningful contributions while learning from other members of the church.
- Participate in events that aren't youth-specific. If your church is hosting an event, don't always assume it's lame. Ask if it would be appropriate to invite students to participate, and encourage other students to join you there.
- Remember, many adults are intimidated by groups of teenagers, especially when they seem closed-off from interacting with the rest of the church. If you're tired of being treated like an immature kid, then try to demonstrate maturity and initiate simple and kind conversations with adults. Exclusively attending youth events or avoiding conversations with adults will only perpetuate this divide between adults and youth.

Digging Deeper

Use these questions for your own personal reflection and journaling, or for discussion with others.

- How old do you think kids should be when they're expected to participate in your church's worship service? Why?
- Why is it important for your spiritual maturity to participate in the church, not just in youth group?

- What's one way you could serve others in your church?
- Share about one person who's at least ten years older than you who's had an impact on your life.

12

How Do Christians Interpret the Old Testament?

W hen you look at your Bible, you'll notice only one binding. One book, all Scripture. As 2 Timothy 3:16–17
famously declares, "All Scripture is breathed out by God and
profitable for teaching, for reproof, for correction, and for train-
ing in righteousness, that the man of God may be complete,
equipped for every good work." It's important to remember that
the Scripture being referred to in these verses is what we call the
Old Testament.

The Bible is one book, composed of both the Old and New
Testaments, equally inspired and authoritative for Christians.
And yet, most Christians have no guilt over enjoying a delicious
lobster even though shellfish is forbidden by Mosaic law. This
raises an important question: how should Christians interpret
the Old Testament in light of the New, and how does this affect
our everyday Christian lives?

SALVATION HISTORY

Christians cannot rightly understand and interpret the Old Testament without a proper understanding of salvation history—the

whole-Bible story of how God saves his people. To review, this one story has four chapters:

1. **Creation: Know where we come from.** God made everything, and it was good, perfect, and holy. People were created in the image of God to worship and serve him as his representatives on earth.

2. **Fall: Know our need.** When Adam and Eve sinned, death spread throughout all of creation. God's image in people remains, but it is fallen and shattered like a broken mirror that still reflects, but with varying degrees of accuracy. All creation groans for redemption.

3. **Redemption: Know how God meets our need.** Time and again throughout Israel's history, God sent saviors, performed saving acts, and established rituals to prepare his people for the coming Savior. Many of these served as figures or "types" that pointed to the one true Savior who would bring redemption. At the right time, Jesus Christ came, lived, and died as the atoning sacrifice for our sin. Through faith in Jesus, we receive new hearts and are adopted as sons and daughters of God. We are united with Christ by the indwelling Holy Spirit who sanctifies and strengthens us in faith and godliness. The New Testament proclaims this gospel and then applies it to show what a godly life looks like.

4. **Glorification: Know where we are headed.** We live in confident expectation that the promise of the new heaven and new earth will not simply restore the garden of Eden, but surpass it (see the description in Revelation 21 and 22). No longer will sin or temptation have any ability to bring about civil war in creation; sin and death will be utterly defeated. This means the fruit of sin is eternally gone. No more death or sorrow or injustice or pain. Everything that has become corrupted and broken will be more than restored; it will be

glorified. God's kingdom will be fully established, and we will live without guilt or shame in the presence of God.

TYPES OF OLD TESTAMENT LAWS

Not all Old Testament laws are the same. This is extremely important to understand. It explains why Christians quote Scripture to say homosexuality is sinful but agree that eating bacon is delicious. The Old Testament laws have traditionally been broken into three categories, each with different implications for the Christian today.

- **Moral law.** These are laws that go back to what it means to be created in the image of God. They should be obeyed and upheld by all people everywhere. This most notably includes the Ten Commandments, all of which are anchored in creation rather than in the formation of Israel. These laws include such moral principles as the hideousness of idolatry, the value of human life, the sacredness of marriage, and the importance of telling the truth.
- **Civil law.** Israel received a set of laws that specifically applied to their nation. Therefore, since we do not live in ancient Israel, these laws do not directly apply to us today. These laws included legal codes, such as punishments for a person who kills his neighbor's cattle. Christians learn basic principles from these laws about what creates a good society and how the Lord wants us to treat others. But they are no longer binding in the same way they were for ancient Israel.
- **Ceremonial law.** Ceremonial laws pertained to the temple, priests, sacrifices, and other aspects of Old Testament worship and cleanliness. Many of these laws overlap with civil law (for example, the dietary code) because Israel's spiritual and civil life were deeply integrated. These laws show us the holiness and purity God requires for acceptable worship, and they reflect God's provision of grace for those who looked forward to the coming Messiah. Because Jesus

is the Lamb of God and our Great High Priest, he is the fulfillment and end of the ceremonial law. We no longer keep it, but we honor its legacy through the way we worship Christ and proclaim the gospel.

USE OF THE LAW FOR CHRISTIANS TODAY

Another helpful distinction is the difference between law and gospel. God's law tells you what you're supposed to do, but the gospel tells you what God has done or has promised to do. *The law gives commands ("Thou shall not . . .") and the gospel gives promises ("There is therefore now no condemnation for those who are in Christ Jesus"[Romans 8:1]).* God's commandments are good and they instruct us in holiness, but God's law has never saved anyone. We are saved by grace, not by works.

If this is true, it's natural to wonder, "Then what's the point? Why pay attention to the law at all, if it doesn't save and only shows me my guilt before God?" Here are three primary purposes of God's law:

1. **The law is a mirror.** When we look into God's law, we come face-to-face with the reality that we are sinners (Romans 7:7). The law cannot rescue us from sin any more than a mirror can wash a dirty face. But without the law, we wouldn't realize our need for ongoing confession, repentance, and grace. If we want to grow in holiness, then recognizing and confessing our sin is pretty important! The law eliminates any claims to self-righteousness and shows us our ongoing need for the grace of God, prompting us to turn to Jesus daily.
2. **The law is a curb.** The law curbs and limits public chaos and preserves social order. God's law promotes what is good for humanity and for creation. Without laws, we would live in anarchy. In this sense, whether someone is a Christian or not, they benefit from God's law because it preserves creation's innate order and social justice.

3. **The law is a guide.** The law also serves as a guide in our holiness. We rely on the commands of God to know what we are progressing toward in sanctification. If we want to know what God expects of us, we should read the law—not only in the Old Testament, but also the commands of the New Testament. It is important to remember that "the law is good if one uses it properly" (1 Timothy 1:8 NIV), that is, if one uses the law as a guide to holiness while relying on the indwelling Holy Spirit for the power to do what the law commands.

This discussion surrounding God's law highlights the perfect righteousness of Jesus. He perfectly kept every commandment, and we are clothed in his active righteousness by faith. In this way, Christians are indeed saved by law-keeping—but not our own. We are saved by the perfect righteousness of Jesus, which is credited to us by faith.

Unfortunately, many Christians consider the Old Testament to be the Word of God while treating it as little more than background information for the gospel. Remember, the Old Testament was Jesus's Bible, it was the Bible of the apostles, and it remains God-breathed Scripture. Read it with confidence, but also with wisdom. Since we are not Israel, not everything is applied to us as directly as other portions of the Old Testament. Read and obey God's laws and promises in light of those to whom they were given and what their function was meant to be. Whether the laws apply directly to us today or not, they remain worthy of our study and attention, for they tell us something about the heart and character of our God who saves.

DIGGING DEEPER

Use these questions for your own personal reflection and journaling, or for discussion with others.

- Do you tend to read the Old or New Testament more often? Is there a reason why?
- What are the four chapters of Salvation History? How would you put the whole-Bible story in your own words?
- What's the difference between the law and gospel?
- How do the different types and functions of the Law help you know how to read the Old Testament better?

13

Should Christians Be Tolerant?

Tolerance is the new golden rule. Worldly tolerance preaches a gospel of unrestrained self-expression. It's a "you do you" culture that encourages people to do or be whatever they think will make them happy. Christians are often labeled as intolerant for stating their convictions and attempting to persuade others of the truth of Scripture. By this worldly definition of tolerance, the only thing that should not be tolerated is intolerance.

I believe a better definition of tolerance is this: respect despite disagreement. This definition acknowledges the disagreement and affirms that both parties want to persuade the other, but insists that the relationship must be marked by mutual respect. Rather than pointing out the irony of intolerance against Christians who affirm historic Christian teaching, it's far more helpful to consider how the gospel leads Christians to love their enemies and pray for those who persecute them.

When the apostles were arguing about who was the greatest, Jesus instructed them to shift their attitudes toward power and authority. The world seeks power through authority, but Christians are called to be servants. Even Jesus described his own mission this way: "the Son of Man did not come to be served, but to serve, and to give his life as a ransom for many" (Matthew

20:28 NIV). Christians are called to live like Christ. When we debate and seek our rights the same way the world does, then our attitude is out of line with the example of Christ.

WHAT TOLERANCE IS (AND ISN'T)

It's common to hear advocates of worldly tolerance quote Jesus in Matthew 7:1, "Do not judge, or you too will be judged" (NIV). And they're right to do so. Quoting Jesus is always a good idea, and Christians shouldn't be known as judges who eagerly bring their verdicts upon the guilty. But this does not mean Jesus is advocating for a "live and let live" version of tolerance. Jesus continues by saying, "How can you say to your brother, 'Let me take the speck out of your eye,' when there is the log in your own eye? You hypocrite, first take the log out of your own eye, and then you will see clearly to take the speck out of your brother's eye" (Matthew 7:4–5 ESV). Jesus's warning is against judging others while being guilty of the very same thing. It is a warning against hypocrisy. His own words say that once his disciples are "able to see clearly" they should help their brother remove the speck from his eye. It is also worth highlighting that Jesus is addressing how brothers—fellow Christians—judge one another. It should not be with a motive to tear down, but to strengthen. Nonbelievers are another matter: we should not expect them to live biblically. They need the gospel, not to be held to a biblical standard they reject. But it is good and right to hold fellow believers to God's Word.

Instead of viewing tolerance as a sinful compromise, Christians see tolerance as an expression of loving their enemies. There are many biblical examples available: Jesus's instruction to go the extra mile, to turn the other cheek, and to pray for those who persecute you—plus Jesus's interactions with lepers, adulterers, and tax collectors. He is gracious and tolerant, but always in a way that invites others into relationship without ignoring their sin.

Yes, Jesus's kind of tolerance assumes disagreement. Otherwise, there's nothing to tolerate. Most people acknowledge this in theory, but practice tolerance as if tolerance equals agreement. Real tolerance is respect despite disagreement.

It is important for us to assume a tolerant posture without buying into the culture's twisted definition of tolerance. This is not a passive-aggressive ceasefire: both groups "putting up with" each other. No one simply wants to be "put up with"! This is a version of tolerance Christians can embrace because it's simply an expression of loving your neighbor—and your enemy—as yourself.

Rules of Engagement for Students in a Tolerant Age

- **Listen, listen, listen.** It is impossible to respect someone you won't listen to. Being a good listener, especially when talking about spiritual things, will show someone you truly value them. Good listeners want to really understand what the other person is saying. They don't merely listen in order to find holes to exploit in the other person's argument. If you are constantly thinking about what you're going to say next in order to win the debate, you aren't listening—you're plotting. Listen first.

- **Repeat back.** If you can't repeat back what the other person just said in a way that they would respond, "Yes, that's what I believe!" you are not ready to voice your disagreement. No one feels respected when someone twists their words and critiques a straw man argument. That is cheap and disrespectful. Instead, ask clarifying questions to make sure you really understand, and demonstrate your respect by repeating back what they just said before you disagree. This often changes the tone from a debate to a conversation.

- **Keep the main thing the main thing.** Jesus is the main thing. What good is it if you present irrefutable evidence about creation or biblical sexuality or whatever else you may be discussing, but the person still rejects the gospel? Those topics are important, but they are not at the heart of what it means to be a Christian. If you are more passionate about debating certain hot topics than you are about presenting the gospel, you have lost sight of the main thing. That said, forcing Jesus into the conversation can sometimes feel like a disingenuous setup. When you are fluent in the language of the gospel and understand how it shapes all of life, you will be able to identify some regular on-ramps (love, hope, identity, etc.) by which the gospel can enter your conversations. And keeping Jesus the main thing in your own heart will keep him the main thing in your conversations too—for he alone gives new life.

Digging Deeper

Use these questions for your own personal reflection and journaling, or for discussion with others.

- Why do Christians have a reputation for being intolerant?
- What do you think about this chapter's definition of tolerance: "Tolerance means respect despite disagreement"?
- How do the biblical examples above shape what Christian tolerance should look like?
- What's the hardest part of the "Rules of Engagement" for you?

14
What Does the Bible Teach about Sex and Dating?

S ex is like fire. Within the proper boundaries of a fireplace it gives light and heat, but unrestrained it causes great harm and can even burn the house down. As teenagers, you are receiving messages about sexuality every day—from the latest Netflix series, from social media, from conversations with friends—and many of those messages contradict one another. Even more concerningly, many teens are getting sex advice from porn sites directly![1] It can be really confusing to know where to turn for reliable advice amid so many conflicting voices, especially when talking with your parents can feel like the most awkward option on the table.

Many assume that Christians believe sex is gross and dirty and sinful, but that's simply not true. One of the reasons God created gender, sex, and marriage was to promote human flourishing. Sexuality is a good and beautiful thing. God did not need to make it feel good, but he did. It is a gift that reflects the delight and pleasure we were created to enjoy through intimacy with our Creator. At the same time, the Bible doesn't pull punches about the dangers of unrestrained sexuality. The cities of Sodom and Gomorrah were destroyed as judgment for their rampant sin and ungodly sexuality. King David, a man after God's own heart, caused great suffering in his family because of his sexual sin against Bathsheba. This is why I believe the fire analogy is helpful when it comes to understanding the biblical teaching about sexuality—it's a good gift that can cause great harm when it's set free from its proper boundaries.

Sex Is for Intimacy

God gave the gift of sex to strengthen intimacy between a husband and a wife. The goal is intimacy—to be fully known without any fear of rejection. This is what so many men and women are trying to attain through their sexual activity, as if sex were a shortcut to it. God created us for intimacy with him and with each other. Sin has brought a deep loneliness into our lives and suspicion into relationships, but sex is a brief moment of joyful acceptance between two partners. Aside from the physical pleasure, this is what makes sex so powerful. And this is why people try using sex as a shortcut to find intimacy with a partner, or to use sex to heal relationships that are deeply broken. But sex was never meant to actually *create* intimacy. It either expresses intimacy by embodying this desire to be "fully known without any fear of rejection" in a very physical way, or it gives a short taste of that acceptance but is quickly replaced by the reminder that you are not fully known.

Singleness can sound like a sentence to lifelong loneliness. This fear drives many into toxic patterns like serial dating, jumping from one relationship into another. But singleness isn't a life sentence to loneliness and depression. After all, Jesus himself was never married. If you think, *Well, he's God, so obviously he'd still be happy and content if he was single*, then consider words the apostle Paul uses while talking about his singleness: "I wish that all of you were as I am" (1 Corinthians 7:7 NIV). Sex is often viewed as the greatest expression of intimacy, as if without it you'll only be a shell of a person. But that's just not true. Sex is an incredibly powerful expression of intimacy, but many single and celibate people (like Jesus, Paul, and countless others who you actually know) have experienced meaningful, nonsexual intimacy through their friendships and relationship with God.

Sex is about intimacy, and perfect intimacy is found only in Jesus Christ who loved us and saved us while we were still enemies. God chose to redeem sinners and adopt them as sons and daughters. If he gave his life for us while we were still his enemies, then truly nothing can separate us from the love of God. Because of the gospel, the Holy Spirit lives in each Christian—whether single or married—and unites him or her to Christ. God is not far away or distant. He is intimately near. Amid today's sexual revolution, it is important to remember that sexual intimacy was always meant to point people to the intimacy with God they were created to enjoy.

WHY DO CHRISTIANS CARE SO MUCH ABOUT SEXUAL PURITY?

I've heard students ask why Christians are so obsessed with sex. These folk believe that Christians are especially committed to making sure people aren't having any. But that's not entirely fair. Let's be honest: our culture as a whole is obsessed with sex. As teenagers, you are bombarded with sexual messages all the time. If the church isn't talking about sex, then it's probably the only place you go that isn't talking about it.

We all know that our sexuality is an important part of our identity. If Christians are people who live to glorify God in everything they do, then surely this includes our sexuality. The apostle Paul addresses Christian sexuality this way,

> "I have the right to do anything," you say—but not everything is beneficial. "I have the right to do anything"—but I will not be mastered by anything. You say, "Food for the stomach and the stomach for food,

and God will destroy them both." The body, however, is not meant for sexual immorality but for the Lord, and the Lord for the body. By his power God raised the Lord from the dead, and he will raise us also. Do you not know that your bodies are members of Christ himself? Shall I then take the members of Christ and unite them with a prostitute? Never! Do you not know that he who unites himself with a prostitute is one with her in body? For it is said, "The two will become one flesh." But whoever is united with the Lord is one with him in spirit." (1 Corinthians 6:12–17 NIV)

It may sound weird to say, but sex is about the gospel. Just as a man and woman are bound together by the covenantal intimacy of marriage, so too the believer is united with Christ through salvation. Marriage joins a husband and wife in a lifelong relationship of affection and commitment, while salvation unites the believer with Christ in this life and into all eternity. Sex is a physical symbol of the spiritual intimacy we were created to experience. This is why treating sex like it's no big deal is such a problem.

Pornography, sexual intercourse before marriage, adultery, and homosexuality are sexual parallels with spirituality that have no affection for or commitment to the triune God. Spiritually speaking, embracing sexual sin is like trying to enjoy the gifts of God while rejecting God himself. Purity in all areas of life should be important to every Christian—even a casual glance at the Bible will make that clear. Christians never have the option to redefine sexuality according to their wants or desires. Instead, Scripture calls us to self-denial and to holiness in all areas of life, including our sexuality. God's will regarding sexuality isn't to limit or restrict your pleasure or enjoyment, but to guard your heart and to help you experience true intimacy.

DATING AND MARRIAGE

If you want to honor God with your life and sexuality, the way you approach dating and marriage matters. Who you marry is one of the most significant decisions you'll ever make. Marrying someone who shares your faith and is well-suited for you will enrich your life in ways that are difficult to overstate. Many Christian youth nod their head in agreement to this statement, and then say, "Yeah, okay. But I'm in high school. That's so far down the road, I'm going to skip this marriage section." Please don't! Your relationships today pave the path for your future relationships. The odds of you marrying your first boyfriend or girlfriend may be slim, but you're building patterns today that affect the types of people you choose to date in the future. The way you treat your partner is incredibly important. Treating your partner with respect, dignity, and honor doesn't automatically happen when you fall in love or say "I do."

Your relationships change you. This is why it's important to be choosy and intentional about who you agree to date and what types of boundaries you establish (and maintain). One of those boundaries should be a shared faith. When you, as a Christian, date a non-Christian, there's a certain level of "like-mindedness" that simply cannot exist. If your values are the same as a non-Christian's, that means yours aren't built on the gospel as much as you think they are.

Trying to find a Christian boyfriend or girlfriend who you "click" with can be a discouraging process. It's better to be single in Christ than to give yourself to someone who doesn't share your faith. I know that can sound harsh, especially if your parents are not both believers. But every mixed-faith marriage I know has endured multiple heartaches when it comes to making significant family decisions. God is gracious, and I don't want to give the impression that these marriages are doomed to be unhappy and miserable. But if you want to live for Christ and glorify him in all areas of life, then that should involve your sexuality and your romantic relationships (2 Corinthians 6:14).

DIGGING DEEPER

Use these questions for your own personal reflection and journaling, or for discussion with others.

- What are some of the differences between the ways you hear Christians talk about sex versus the ways you hear non-Christians talk about it?
- How do people use sex as a shortcut for intimacy?
- Put into your own words what this chapter says about sexual intimacy as a reflection of our relationship with God.
- How does a biblical foundation for sexual intimacy and marriage affect the way you approach dating and relationships now?

15
What Does the Bible Teach about LGBTQ+ Issues?

It's tempting to avoid discussing LGBTQ+ issues because of how challenging it is to navigate well. But this is an unavoidable topic for most teenagers every day. A survey from the Barna Group and Impact 360 reveals that 33 percent of teenagers believe a person's gender is determined by what the person feels rather than their birth sex.[1] Roughly one in five people in GenZ identifies as LGBTQ+—lesbian, gay, bisexual, transgender, or queer—nearly triple that of the rest of the US population.[2]

The goal of this chapter is not to present a complete defense of historic Christian sexuality, but to offer short responses to the big questions. I also hope this chapter can model the Christian tolerance discussed in chapter 13. The effects of sin have corrupted everything in this world—from droughts to earthquakes, from cancer to mental illness. This also includes our sexual and gender identities. It is essential to remember, despite all the controversy and passion surrounding the LGBTQ+ conversation, that everyone's greatest need is the same: to be reconciled with God through faith in Jesus Christ—and that invitation must remain the priority. The greatest good is not to turn gay people straight or transgender people cisgender, but that each person would respond to the invitation of Jesus Christ, and that he would sanctify us all according to the patient work of the Holy Spirit.

WHAT DOES THE BIBLE SAY ABOUT HOMOSEXUALITY?

As the last chapter emphasized, the Bible teaches that sex is a gift intended to express intimacy. It's a mirror that reflects the believer's union with Christ in perfect intimacy. This union involves two partners who are different from one another—a human and God. As Christians, we are "the Bride of Christ," wedded to Christ our "bridegroom" (Ephesians 5:25–27; Revelation 19:7–9). Homosexual relationships cannot reflect this human–divine relationship because they bring together two same-sex people. This is the theological foundation for the Bible's teaching on homosexuality.

The first command that God gave to humanity was to "be fruitful and multiply" (Genesis 1:28). Yes, that involves more than making babies, but it cannot involve less than that. God's design for human reproduction means something. Even if you only believe in evolution, a culture that embraces homosexuality cannot sustain and reproduce itself apart from modern medicine.

The Bible explicitly calls homosexual acts sinful in verses like Leviticus 18:22, Romans 1:26–27, 1 Corinthians 6:9–11 and in others. Some LGBTQ+ advocates have argued that these references that forbid same-sex relationships aren't about homosexuality but are against ritual pedophilia in the temples—but that's simply not the case. Sexual activity with children is obviously unbiblical and is also included in what those passages condemn. But a basic reading of the text is clear, and many advocates admit that the Bible does not condone LGBTQ+ lifestyles.

It's also common to wonder why Christians continue to say homosexuality is a sin while they eat lobster and wear mixed-textile clothing. Isn't that hypocritical and inconsistent? That's not the case, because not every commandment in the Torah (first five books of the Old Testament) is the same. As discussed earlier in chapter 12, there are different types of Old Testament laws. Some of the commandments were given for ritual sacrifices, while others were for civil life to help determine Israel's court of law, and others had to do with God's commandments for what it means to live a good and righteous life. Christ fulfilled the ritual law. We don't follow the civil law because we aren't living in biblical Israel, but we are still human beings, so the moral law remains as the guardrail for our holiness. Our gender and sexuality are about what it means to be human, not merely about how we choose to express ourselves. This is why the commands about sexuality are considered part of the moral law (which applies to all people) rather than the civil law (which was particular to Israel).

It is important to emphasize that while homosexual activity (which includes the sin of lustful desire) is sinful, same-sex sin is not inherently more sinful than heterosexual sin. Everyone, regardless of sexual orientation, is called to resist temptation, practice self-denial, and pursue holiness.

WHAT DOES THE BIBLE SAY ABOUT GENDER?

Today's gender conversation is a redefinition of what it means to be human. That's not a small thing. There have always been people on the fringes of society who embraced nontraditional gender roles, but no other generation throughout human history has been so bold as to reject male and female gender distinctions. Statements like "I have a uterus and I am not a woman" are genuinely new and radical. Previous generations would have thought it unthinkable to give hormone blockers and offer breast-removal surgery to teenagers. And yet it is increasingly common for those who affirm historic Christian teaching on gender and sexuality to be ostracized and canceled.

When God created man and woman he did not merely call them "good," as he did with everything else he created (Genesis 1:4–25). He called the creation of man and woman "very good"

(Genesis 1:31). It's important to emphasize that while God created man and woman, and while the Bible offers some basic guidelines for manhood and womanhood, many of our social norms aren't mentioned in Scripture. It's not sinful for girls to be tomboys or for boys to be sensitive. Older generations may talk about our cultural expectations for men and women as if they're clearly defined by Scripture, but surprisingly little is explicitly commanded. Cultures around the world have different attitudes and behaviors that are considered "normal," and that's okay. But male and female gender remains foundational to what it means to be a human being, made in the image of God.

Gender dysphoria is a clinical condition where a person suffers distress because their sex and gender identity are in conflict. This is a real condition and should be treated with utmost seriousness, but this does not mean it should be affirmed in order to "support" the person who experiences it.[3] The number of teenagers (especially teenage girls) who have been diagnosed with gender dysphoria is an epidemic and should lead us to ask honest and critical questions.[4] Why is this suddenly so common among GenZ when it has been present but rare throughout previous generations? Why is gender dysphoria particularly common in countries with high social media access? How many people transition and later de-transition, and how should that affect the treatments we offer at various ages? These are honest questions that have sadly become unacceptable to ask in today's culture.[5]

A transgender identity isn't primarily about sexuality, but about what it means to be human. Christians do not deny the reality of gender dysphoria any less than we deny the reality of deep-seated homosexual desires or other medical and mental health diagnoses. But natural desires are not automatically good and beneficial for us because our human nature has been innately corrupted by the curse in Genesis 3:14–19. Those who struggle with their sexual and gender identity remain beloved friends who carry the image of God. They are worthy of love, respect, and mutual understanding. There is absolutely no room for violence or hate or mockery or coarse joking. Christians should follow Jesus's example toward tax collectors and adulterers, inviting them into abundant life and away from their sin.

Aren't All Sins the Same?

Everyone is a sinner. No one can engage in conversations about LGBTQ+ issues from a place of superiority. As Jesus says to the crowd surrounding a woman caught in adultery, "Let any one of you who is without sin be the first to throw a stone at her" (John 8:7 niv). As tempting as it may be to treat homosexuality as a greater sin than other forms of sexual immorality (pornography, adultery, and sex outside of marriage), all sexual sin is equally wrong.

It's true that all sin is equally wrong, but that doesn't mean all sin is the same. I bet you'd rather be slapped in the face or lied to than murdered. Both are wrong, but it's just plain false to say they're equally bad. Similarly, the Old Testament commanded different types of sacrifices to atone for different kinds of sins and offenses. The Bible never treats all sins as if they're equal. But what the Bible does teach is that all sin is a serious offense against God.

First Corinthians 6:18 is particularly clear about the serious nature of sexual sin: "Flee from sexual immorality. Every other sin a person commits is outside the body, but the sexually immoral person sins against his own body." It's important to note this passage doesn't differentiate between different types of sexual sin, but it does clearly state that sexual sin is different from other sins. Therefore, we should make every grace-fueled effort to flee from it rather than minimizing its danger by saying, "What's the big deal? All sin is the same."

Biblically speaking, adultery is routinely equated with idolatry. This is because marriage is intended to express the intimacy people were created to have with God—two partners who are similar but different from each other, in loving union together.

Adultery not only disrupts marriage, but also represents people who cheat on God with other gods and idols. Along these lines, homosexuality would represent atheism because it involves two same-sex people rather than a complementary partnership between the sexes. This is why Romans 1:26–27 uses homosexuality as an example of people's spiritual rejection of God in favor of worldliness.

Can You Be a LGBTQ+ Christian?

A common question is whether or not someone can embrace a homosexual or transgender lifestyle and still be a Christian. A Christian's identity is first and foremost shaped by their relationship with God through Jesus Christ, so I am uncomfortable with combining *any* other adjective with the label Christian. When we do that, there is a subtle competition between the two identities. The Christian's identity as a Christian should be the core identity that reshapes and refines every other identifier: gender, nationality, sexuality, cultural preferences, denominational affiliations, etc. These other identifiers may be valid and important, but they must be shaped by God and by the authority of Scripture rather than the other way around.

The Bible does not affirm homosexual activity, and it teaches us that a person's sex and gender are assigned by our wise and loving God at birth. Christians who live with gender dysphoria or same-sex attraction embrace their identity in Christ as their primary identity rather than allowing their sexuality to be the most important thing about them. This is often a confusing and difficult road for them, and it's important to ensure they don't walk it alone. These friends need our patient and loving support as we lead them to Jesus over the long haul.

The call of the gospel is an invitation to a new life through grace-fueled repentance. A new believer will not repent of every sin immediately; it is a lifelong journey that requires much grace (from God and from others!). But Christians do repent eventually. The Holy Spirit is at work in their hearts, persuading them of the goodness and truthfulness of God's Word—even when it brings conviction of sin. Those who profess faith in Christ Jesus but never repent of sin show that, although they may be trying to gain the treasures of heaven, they don't really want new life as a child of God. The timeline for this repentance may take years because of the complex nature of sexual sin. Be generous in longsuffering with LGBTQ+ friends. If a practicing homosexual or transgender person professes to be a Christian and yet persists in rejecting the Bible's teaching on sexuality, that person's conversion remains questionable.

But rather than lobbing this warning as a grenade, offer concern that reflects the gospel. It is not a cop-out to leave judgment in God's hands. The Lord has not rushed into judgment, and neither should you. So, when in doubt, err on the side of patience. At the same time, remember it is not loving or gracious to affirm a professing Christian's sinful lifestyle, regardless of what that particular sin may be.

DIGGING DEEPER

Use these questions for your own personal reflection and journaling, or for discussion with others.

- How would you put what the Bible teaches about homosexuality into your own words?
- This chapter claims, "A transgender identity isn't necessarily about sexuality, but about what it means to be human." Do you agree or disagree, and why?
- How does adultery theologically represent idolatry, and how does homosexuality theologically represent atheism?
- How would you respond to someone who says all sins are the same, so Christians should stop worrying about gender and sexuality?

16

Can Christians Believe in Evolution?

Many of us live with the assumption that science and faith cannot coexist. Often, this is reinforced by youth groups that either completely avoid conversations about creation and evolution or discuss it in a way that dismisses scientific claims as an atheistic agenda. But that's not the way it has to be. Consider the glory of creation and the complexity of understanding how God created it, while holding some convictions about science:

First, science is good. Sadly, the stereotype of religious folk is that we are unscientific or even anti-science. And yet, most of Western history's greatest scientists were faithful Christians who practiced science as a way to explore God's good creation—consider Johannes Kepler, Galileo, Francis Bacon, and Isaac Newton, to name only a few. Today, however, many people have replaced faith in God with naturalism, which says, "If I can't physically and scientifically prove it, then it isn't real." A naturalistic worldview has no place among those who profess to worship Jesus, but Christians are not opposed to science. Instead, Christians view scientific studies as an exploration of the incredible world God created.

Second, research leads to multiple interpretations. There isn't always one clear and obvious conclusion to scientific inquiries, and scientists often draw different interpretations from the same information. The popular voice isn't always correct. Without room to debate interpretations, the voice that affirms what people want to believe will often win the public opinion. Scientific research and debate are good on every level, and it is good for Christians to participate in genuine scientific inquiry.

Third, science is limited to exploring fields of research within its own boundaries. This means science cannot fully know something beyond the natural world. This is a built-in limitation naturalism needs to acknowledge. Expecting science to reveal something beyond the limits of science is irrational.

Fourth, even the most literal creationist agrees there is some adaptation within species. Adaptation and evolution *within* species make clear scientific sense. For example, dogs with thick fur will endure colder climates better than shorthair breeds.[1] The evolution debate revolves around whether or not one species can evolve into a whole new species, not whether or not one species can adapt and evolve at all. With these guiding convictions in mind, let's consider some of the most common views of creation.

SUMMARY OF POPULAR VIEWS ABOUT CREATION

1. **Young-earth creation:** God created the earth in six 24-hour days. Genesis 1 and 2 use the word "day" to mean a 24-hour day and should be taken at face value. The earth is thousands (not millions or billions) of years old. Adam and Eve were historical people whom God specially made in his image, and who sinned and were then sent out of the garden.

2. **Old-earth creation:** God created the earth, but not in 24-hour days. Genesis 1 and 2 describe what God did but not precisely how he did it, so there's some room for science to fill in the details God left out of the biblical account. The

earth is probably very old, but Adam and Eve were historical people whom God specially made in his image, and who
sinned and were then sent out of the garden.

3. **Framework hypothesis:** Genesis 1 is not an account in-
tending to tell *how* God created the world (in what order
or how long he took), but a poetic way to teach *why*. This
view highlights that the Bible's creation account is laid out
to teach us that a Creator King built a kingdom, populated
it, and placed men and women to rule over it.[2] With this interpretation there is much room for scientific explanations
of how God did this. Most framework proponents view
Genesis 2 as historical, meaning Adam and Eve were historical people who were specially and distinctly created by
God in his image, and who sinned and were then sent out
of the garden.

4. **Theistic evolution:** God initiated and used evolution to
create humanity. Theistic evolution can encompass a wide
range of views, all generally holding to some form of old-
earth creation, with some going so far as to claim God didn't
personally oversee the evolutionary process but merely set it
up to happen naturally. According to this view, Adam and
Eve are not viewed as historic people. Instead, they are symbolic figures who describe humanity's sinful condition and
rebellion against God. (Theistic evolution is a broad camp,
so these descriptions may not apply to all its adherents).

WHAT CHRISTIANS MUST AFFIRM ABOUT CREATION

In all these discussions about creation and evolution, it's tempting to be overwhelmed and shout with exasperation, "Why
does this matter? I give up!" It's frustratingly common to hear
people talk as if there's only one *true* Christian view of creation.
That's not true, but there are a few foundational truths the Bible
teaches that serve as the foundation of a biblical view of creation.

God created. "In the beginning, God created the heavens
and the earth" (Genesis 1:1). However creation happened, it

is because God caused it. The creation of the world took place by the personal will and love of God. Because God created the world, he is worthy of worship. We worship Jesus Christ, the incarnate Word who spoke creation into existence (John 1:1–14). Our Savior is also the giver of life.

God created man and woman in his image. "So God created man in his own image, in the image of God he created him; male and female he created them" (Genesis 1:27). Humanity is not a happy accident. We are special among all creation because God specifically set us apart to reflect his glory on the earth. Because we are formed in the image of God, we represent him. We are not here for our own glory, to create monuments to ourselves, or to take advantage of others and the earth God created. Instead, we are placed here to reflect his divine nature and to represent him in all creation. This includes cultivating, caring for, and building on the earth for God's glory and the good of all. God is the Creator, and so we create. God is the giver of life, and so we promote life. God is the Savior of creation, and so we forgive and restore what has been broken. When we feel worthless and like utter failures, we can remember in whose image we were created. Additionally, understanding the ways God's image has been broken within us because of sin will empower us to repent of sin and believe that the gospel restores the image of Christ in us (Ephesians 4:17–24).

Adam and Eve are historic people. The account of Adam and Eve is never mentioned in Scripture as anything other than historical and reliable. Even when some symbolism is referenced, it is anchored in Adam and Eve's historic sin and its effects upon all creation. Adam is a symbolic figurehead for all humanity (Romans 5:12–18; 1 Corinthians 15:45–48). His historicity (and that of the first sin) is crucial to salvation history—otherwise God's wrath toward his fallen creation becomes a metaphor rather than a real problem in need of a real Savior. The story of humanity flows from Adam and Eve being real, historical people whose sin and promised salvation continue to impact our lives today.

DIGGING DEEPER

Use these questions for your own personal reflection and journaling, or for discussion with others.

- Why do you think Christianity has a reputation for being anti-science?
- Which of the Christian viewpoints on creation seems most convincing to you? Why?
- Why is it important for Christians to affirm that God actually created Adam and Eve, rather than allowing for evolution as the process that eventually led to our first ancestors?
- How do the essentials of Christian creationism help you know what to emphasize in conversations with others?

17

How Should Christians Think about Mental Health Struggles?

ecent statistics suggest nearly one-third of students who read this book regularly struggle with anxiety and depression, while two-thirds consider it a major concern among their peers.[1] Everyone walks through sad or anxious seasons in life, but many are experiencing something deeper and more overwhelming: a sense of despair with no hope for improvement. If this is true of you, dear reader, then I want you to know you can find the hope and strength to endure in Christ.

Many of us ask, "Does faith in God help me with my mental health diagnosis?" It does! But affirming the power of the gospel for those who suffer from mental health diagnoses does not mean we should overlook the legitimate and complicated factors and treatments for these diagnoses. With this in mind, it is helpful to have a basic understanding of the most common mental health diagnoses and how the gospel shapes those who have received a diagnosis. This will prevent the temptation to reply to mental health struggles by quoting a Bible verse and saying, "Have more faith and try harder."

Mental health is nothing new, even if it's a term the older generations did not use. Look no further than the Psalms: "Why, my soul, are you downcast? Why so disturbed within me?" (Psalm 43:5 NIV). Elijah was crippled by anxiety and depression when God spoke to him in a soft voice (1 Kings 19). If faith eliminated mental health struggles, there would be fewer psalms expressing how anxiety and depression can plague those who trust in God.

IS IT OKAY FOR CHRISTIANS TO TAKE MEDICATION FOR MENTAL HEALTH?

Some Christians wonder if it is faithless to take medication for mental health disorders. Most people know Christians who minimize the seriousness of mental health struggles by encouraging those who suffer to simply pray more. While every Christian would benefit from a more committed prayer life, this advice is often given in a dismissive manner that communicates that the friend's suffering is due to a lack of faith. But the corrective to this false view is not a wholesale embrace of all medicine as a pharmaceutical savior, either. Instead, Christian wisdom has us come alongside one another with gospel-bought hope and patient friendship that flows from a robust view of sin's effects on humanity.

Mental health problems are one element of the fallenness we endure in this world that awaits restoration in the new heaven and new earth. Until then, Christians cling to the gospel even while they take their medicine. Medicine is a gift from God and should be viewed as a providential means of help for those who suffer. It should not be a Christian's first response when faced with a potential mental health diagnosis, but it also shouldn't be a mark of shame. Whether the medicine is to help with anxiety, depression, ADHD, OCD, or some other diagnosis, our Savior's name is Jesus Christ. He is the one who brings true hope for healing and restoration, even while we take our medicine with breakfast in the morning.

COMMON MENTAL HEALTH DIAGNOSES

Chances are good that either you or one of your friends struggles with anxiety or depression or an eating disorder. I hope
these definitions and basic descriptions will give you tools to ask
for help and assist your friends in asking for help too.

- **Anxiety.** Every person has experienced anxiety. Jesus directly
  addresses it in Matthew 6:25–34 when he repeatedly says,
  "Do not be anxious." Christians are called to live by faith,
  not in anxiety. Most people experience elevated stress (which
  often presents as anxiety) during particularly challenging
  circumstances, whether it is a big test, conflict with friends,
  or tryouts for a sports team or theatrical performance. But
  this is not the same thing as clinical anxiety. *Generalized
  anxiety disorder* (GAD) includes an overwhelming feeling
  of dread over life in general (not over any particular event
  or issue) for an extended period of time. *Panic disorder*
  occurs when a person periodically experiences anxiety with
  physical symptoms that may feel like a heart attack—racing
  pulse, sweating, and/or chest tightening. *Social anxiety
  disorder* happens when someone either worries about the
  social repercussions of their anxiety so much that they avoid
  social interaction, or when they experience feelings similar
  to panic while in social situations.
- **Depression.** Similar to anxiety, depression is something
  many people experience for a season after something painful
  or difficult happens in their life. When depression lasts for
  a prolonged period or if it leaves a person feeling like life
  isn't worth living anymore, then it's time to consult a mental
  health expert. The range of symptoms for depression in
  teenagers can vary widely, so it's most important to look for
  significant behavior changes. When they suddenly become
  lethargic and unmotivated, or high-strung with sudden
  outbursts of anger, it's important to pay careful attention. It

is also important to notice how they talk about themselves and about the value of life. Especially encourage them to seek professional help if you fear a friend or loved one is heading toward self-harm. If you or someone you know needs help, please contact the Suicide Lifeline by calling or texting 988 on any phone.

- **Eating disorders.** Eating disorders often hide beneath anxiety and depression, so it is important to know some warning signs. *Anorexia* is a disorder in which someone significantly restricts their food intake, sometimes to the point of not eating for extensive periods of time. *Bulimia* usually involves a cycle of binge eating and then purging through vomiting or use of laxatives. There are other eating disorders, too, like *orthorexia*—a disruptive obsession with healthy eating. Today's youth culture—with its obsession over appearances and the prevalence of social media—provides fertile soil for negative body image. It's important for parents and friends to be on the lookout for these disorders and to help others develop a biblical view of the body.

RESPONDING TO MENTAL HEALTH STRUGGLES

When you are struggling with your mental health, look for faithful mentors who can come alongside you to listen, weep, laugh, and remind you of the glorious promise you have because Jesus rose from the grave and overcame the curse of sin. Remember, your parents do want what's best for you; talk with them about your concerns too. If you think that conversation would be easier with a youth leader or other mentor present, then ask if they'd be willing to mediate.

The gospel gives hope for today ("God still loves me and he is with me") and hope for the future ("God will make everything right"). In John 10:10, Jesus says, "The thief comes only to steal and kill and destroy. I came that they may have life and have it abundantly." When you struggle with your mental health, it's important to lift your eyes to see the cross as a clear demonstration of God's love. Jesus understands your fears and anxiety from the inside, not merely as an observer. He himself experienced the sadness of grief (John 11:35), temptation (Matthew 4:1–11), and anxiety (Luke 22:44). The battle for mental health can easily lead into shame and insecurity, but the gospel invites you to receive the loving-kindness of God and assures you that your worth is secure because of God's promise.

May the next generation increasingly discover the abundant life that comes by the gracious hand of the Good Shepherd. Faith in Jesus does not promise a smooth road and to fix life's trials, but God promises his presence, love, and eternal hope because of the empty tomb. This is a message worth remembering daily.

DIGGING DEEPER

Use these questions for your own personal reflection and journaling, or for discussion with others.

- Why do you think some Christians have a hard time talking about mental health?
- How do verses like Psalm 43:3 and 1 Kings 19 (both referenced above) comfort you in knowing that even biblical heroes faced mental health struggles?
- How can the gospel give you hope when you're facing a mental health struggle?
- Why is it important to talk with someone about your struggles with mental health?

18

Does Committing Suicide Condemn You to Hell?

This question sobers me whenever I'm asked because of the complicated reasons why students ask it. There are two sad reasons teenagers ask this question: they have a friend or loved one who recently committed suicide and they are grieving over that person's eternal fate, or they themselves are quietly wrestling with suicide as their own escape plan for the trials of this life. If you are personally facing either of these issues, then you may want to hold off on reading this chapter until you're in a more stable place with your mental health. Most importantly, if you are experiencing suicidal thoughts, please talk to a parent or another trusted adult for help, or call the National Suicide Hotline at 1-800-273-8255 or 988. God's promise to be with and guard you is more trustworthy than your feelings. Even when you do not feel God's presence or love, he is caring for you in ways you simply cannot perceive in the moment. In every challenge of life, you can find hope and comfort in God's promise that sinners can become the dearly loved children of God through faith in Jesus Christ.

God is the author and giver of life. Death is also in God's hands. Taking a life is murder—whether it's someone else's life or one's own. Life is a gift to treasure and protect, and suicide is self-murder. With this understanding in mind, let's consider whether or not someone who committed suicide could still have been a real Christian, and whether or not suicide automatically condemns a person to hell.

THE UNFORGIVABLE SIN?

Two questions often arise regarding professed Christians who commit suicide: First, could they be saved when they did not have the opportunity to confess their sin and seek forgiveness? Second, did they commit blasphemy, the unforgivable sin?

Regarding the opportunity to confess, passages like Romans 6:10 and Hebrews 10:10 make it clear that Christ died "once for all." This means that once a person has repented of their sin and placed their faith in Christ (see chapters one and two), all of that Christian's sin has already been atoned for—past, present, and future sin. When a Christian receives the grace of God, it is full grace. So just like Christians who die while committing any other sin (maybe they died while lying), Christians who commit suicide have indeed sinned, but their Savior remains greater than their sin. Faith in Jesus Christ, not perfect confession of every specific sin we commit, is what saves.

On the matter of the unforgivable sin, suicide is not that sin. The sin of blasphemy against the Holy Spirit is mentioned in Matthew 12:31 and is best described as a defiant rejection of the gospel. It is the rejection of the Spirit's prompting to believe that Christ is Lord and that God raised him from the grave. All who by faith confess Christ as Lord and profess him as Savior will be saved, for this is the work of the Holy Spirit in a sinner's life. While friends and family will struggle with their loved one's suicide for obvious reasons, there is no biblical reason to believe those who die by suicide have automatically forfeited their salvation.

Those who profess Jesus Christ as Lord but commit suicide have, at least in that final moment, lost sight of the truth of the gospel. The gospel declares that a Christian is united to Christ in this very life. In the midst of the pain and anguish of life, it is imperative for Christians to be reminded of this glorious truth: the love God the Father gives to God the Son is the very same love that is delivered to the Christian through the indwelling Holy Spirit. To say it another way, God loves us with the same love that he gives to Jesus. This is not a cheap answer or an easy fix.

Life is hard, and mental illness is a tragic reality in this fallen world. Anyone can fall into a spiritually dark place where their eyes have lost sight of God's face. God will not waste this difficult season in your life. Ultimately, the gospel remains good news: Christians can live with hope because Jesus rose from the grave, ascended into glory, and will indeed return to complete the restoration of all things. This is the message of hope for every Christian to cling to in their darkest moments.

So, the answer to the question is yes, those who commit suicide could have still been real Christians. Christians who profess faith in Jesus and then commit suicide do not do so in order to claim gospel promises, but because they have lost sight of them. In the midst of these difficult issues, we joyfully lift our eyes to Jesus with trust and confidence that we can live this life with hope, peace, and love.

How to Help a Friend who is Experiencing Suicidal Thoughts

It's become increasingly and heartbreakingly common for teenagers to fall into deep depressions that involve self-harm and suicidal thoughts. If this describes you, please talk with a parent, school guidance counselor, or another trusted adult. Getting help is an act of courage, not weakness.

If you have a friend or some other acquaintance who has made comments in person or online about self-harm or suicidal thoughts, please take this seriously. Good friends often try their best to care for each other and counsel one another, but sometimes good friends need to care enough to tell someone else. Share your concern with your own parents, or with theirs, or with another trustworthy adult at school or church. Don't take the burden to "save" them onto your own shoulders. Be their friend, not their savior or therapist. Encourage them to ask for help, perhaps even offering to be with them while talking to their parents. There are no easy rules for how to comfort and minister to parents or students who may be suicidal or are grieving after a suicide.

The following is presented to help you support friends who are struggling:

Pray for wisdom and be a friend. God is generous to those who ask (James 1:5). Be careful about what advice you give, because you're a friend, not a mentor or therapist. Don't underestimate the importance of friendship during seasons like this. Beware of making every conversation about their struggles. Even when you don't know what to say, simply being present is a meaningful gift to friends who are struggling. Pray for wisdom about how to be a good friend, and resist the temptation to take it upon yourself to "fix" them. Be confident in God, seek his wisdom, and simply be a friend.

Remember the gospel is more than a ticket to heaven. The gospel is the Christian's foundation for peace when they suffer ("Christ has overcome!"), joy when they are anxious ("You are dearly loved by your heavenly Father"), comfort when they are in danger ("Greater is he who is in you than he who is in the world"), and assurance of love when they feel unlovable ("Christ died for us while we were still sinners"). Pray for opportunities to invite your friends to receive the new life and hope that come through faith in Jesus Christ.

Ask gentle but direct questions about their intentions. Your tone and body language matter—a welcoming posture means you are finding the place where gentleness and directness overlap. If a friend is making jokes or other comments about self-harm, then you may want to clearly and directly ask, "Are you thinking about hurting yourself?" This question will also open up a conversation about why you're asking and will communicate how much you genuinely care for them. Yes, it's awkward and uncomfortable, but you may never realize how much it means to them that you cared enough to ask the question.

Get your friend the necessary help. If they confess that they might hurt themselves, talk to a trusted adult (like a teacher, guidance counselor, parent, or youth leader) as soon as possible and ask them to contact the authorities for your friend to receive help. You cannot shoulder the responsibility to "fix" your friend, but in extreme circumstances your efforts to raise the alarm could make all the difference in their world. Finally, if you or someone you know needs help, please contact the Suicide Lifeline by calling or texting 988 on any phone.

DIGGING DEEPER

Use these questions for your own personal reflection and journaling, or for discussion with others.

- Does the Bible teach suicide is the unforgivable sin?
- How do you decide when to tell someone else about a friend's suicidal comments?
- Some people might view the gospel as an escape hatch from life's struggles. How is this a significant misunderstanding of what the gospel is all about?
- Why should Christians continue to endure through hardship rather than see suicide as an escape from life's struggles?

19

Why Pray If God Will Do What He Wants?

Prayer is an integral part of the Christian life. God's people are instructed to intercede for others (2 Corinthians 1:11) and to make their requests known to God (Psalm 17:6). Christians pray with confidence, knowing that God is their heavenly Father who delights in giving good gifts to his children (Matthew 7:11) and that "if we ask anything according to his will he hears us" (1 John 5:14). Yet many people wonder why they should bother praying if God is sovereign—that is, in complete control over all things. If you struggle with this question, I invite you to think of it as an excellent opportunity to wrestle with the Bible and apply it to your daily faith.

We Pray Because God Is Sovereign

Although this chapter title reflects the way people usually ask this question, it reveals a fundamental misunderstanding of God's sovereignty. God's sovereignty isn't just a power play for him to always get his own way. We should first recognize that the value of prayer isn't canceled by God's sovereignty, but actually depends on it. After all, if God is *not* sovereign, why pray at all? We pray and plead with God to grant our requests, like children plead with their father, because he is fully able to grant our requests.

For example, consider how we pray for the salvation of our friends. Ephesians 2:8 tells us salvation comes from God: "This is not your own doing; it is the gift of God." Similarly, 1 Timothy 2:4 encourages us to pray for all people because God "desires all people to be saved." In his sovereignty, God invites us to pray for our friends and family and enemies precisely *because* God is sovereign. Rather than giving into skepticism or discouragement ("I've shared the gospel with them so many times, they'll never believe in Jesus!"), our prayers are fueled by confidence that God can truly change the most hardened hearts and stubborn wills.

If, as some say, "God is a gentleman," then he would simply be a bystander who looks on as humans write their own destinies, occasionally shouting advice from the bleachers. Instead, the Bible paints a different portrait: God is intimately and personally involved in calling, empowering, and using people to accomplish his good and perfect will. God's sovereignty gives us courage to pray, because our God hears us and is able to deliver.

WE PRAY BECAUSE WE ARE GOD-DEPENDENT WORSHIPPERS

We pray as an acknowledgment that we are not independent creatures. We depend on God, who provides. We are God's children, not slaves, employees, or strangers who are nagging him into giving us what we want. We come to him with requests, prayers, and offerings of thanksgiving and praise as a natural overflow of our relationship. Rather than coming before God to boss him around (like the clay shouting at the potter in Isaiah 45:9), we pray because we trust God as our loving, heavenly Father. This is why prayer becomes a struggle in those seasons when we lose sight of our need for God and instead begin to rely on our own ability to provide. Prayer is at the core of the Christian's relationship with God because it's the relational connection with God that builds, nurtures, and reinforces faith.

God does not always grant our requests. When that happens, it's an opportunity for us to remember why we pray—to practice faith in our heavenly Father, even when his answer to our request is no. Those instances can easily tempt us to think about prayer as a battle between our desires and God's. It is good to bring our requests before God, but if our prayers are only full of requests, we have turned God into little more than a magical genie who's there to do our bidding.

CAST YOUR PRAYERS

It can be confusing to know how to pray, especially if you know that prayer isn't entirely about telling God what you want from him. In Scripture, we see prayers of confession (Psalm 51), praise (Psalm 150), requests for help (Philippians 4:6), intercession for others (James 5:15), and thanksgiving (Psalm 34:1–8). The following is a memorable pattern for prayer that has been laid out a few different ways—ACTS is the best known. Switching up the order may help provide consistency while also keeping your prayers from becoming too routine.

- **Confession.** Confessing your sin to God is important— not because he doesn't know about it already, but because naming your sin and reminding yourself that you have been forgiven is at the heart of the Christian life. When we only pray generic confessions ("Thank you for forgiving me of my sin"), then we can still feel burdened and weighed down by our sin. But when we actually confess our sins ("I know I shouldn't have gossiped about Mary today. Thank you for your grace. Please help me to avoid those conversations and to be known as someone who builds others up."), the power of guilt and shame are washed away by the grace of Christ.
- **Adoration.** God is holy. You are not. When you pray, it's important to remember who you're actually praying to. God is not your buddy, and prayer shouldn't become so casual

that it's nothing special. When you pray, declare who God is and worship him through prayer. Adore him for who he is ("God you are holy and omnipresent and in control of all things") and for what he's done ("You are the God of love who has saved me through Jesus!").

- **Supplication.** God delights in providing for his children. Ask God to supply for your needs. Again, this isn't because God is unaware, but because it's a time for you to remember through prayer that everything you have (and don't have) is by God's gracious and fatherly hand. He is a heavenly Father who delights in giving good gifts to his children. He is also a wise Father who knows what things we don't need (even though we may think we really do!). Prayers of supplication help you walk by faith by recalibrating what you think you need and don't need.

- **Thanksgiving.** How often do we gripe and complain about unanswered prayers without celebrating all the prayers God has fulfilled? Take some time to think about your day and your week, and offer specific prayers of thanksgiving to God ("Father, thank you for my friends—for Kevin, Clark, and Dan. They make my life so much richer and more joyful. What a gift you've given me through them.").

Digging Deeper

Use these questions for your own personal reflection and journaling, or for discussion with others.

- Why might people doubt the value of prayer because of God's sovereignty?
- This chapter argues that God's sovereignty is actually the reason we can pray with confidence. How would you explain this in your own words?
- When you pray, do you pray with confidence or uncertainty about whether or not God is actually listening and responsive?

- How does CAST help you think differently about prayer? Which of these do you already practice most often? Which do you practice least often?

20
Why Does God Allow Suffering?

Another school shooting. A classmate dies in a senseless car accident. A teenage friend is diagnosed with cancer. A tornado causes significant damage in town. Why? Why does God allow these things to happen?

Some Christians respond, "He doesn't. We allow suffering to happen by not being the church. If the church acted like the church, suffering would cease." At first glance, this resonates and seems helpful. It comforts, because it allows us to continue worshipping God without blaming him for evil. It inspires, because it motivates us to alleviate the suffering of others. But it's also empty, because it doesn't address persecution or cancer or earthquakes or random accidents that cannot be prevented by the church "being the church." It also suggests that suffering is always opposed to God's will, and yet Scripture consistently presents suffering as the context for our sanctification and God's glory (Psalm 27; James 1:21; Peter 1:6–7). And in an attempt to let God off the hook, it sets him in the bleachers as an onlooker rather than as the sovereign one who daily sustains his creation, even in the midst of great suffering.

If you're struggling with the question, Why do bad things happen to good people, then welcome to the club. This is something people have been asking since the very beginning. As difficult and confusing as it may be, we want to be sure we're talking about suffering the way the Bible talks about suffering. God is in sovereign control, and people are responsible for their actions. Sometimes suffering happens for no obvious reason other than the reality that all creation has fallen under the curse of sin, and we aren't in the garden of Eden anymore.

LEARNING FROM HABAKKUK AND JOB

Unraveling God's mysterious purposes for suffering can seem like an impossible task. We will never fully understand why God does and allows certain things. Sometimes Christians are tempted to settle for easy answers or to quote a Bible verse as if that'll make the struggle to accept suffering easier. But that's not the way the Bible actually addresses suffering. In one of my favorite books of the Bible, a prophet named Habakkuk comes before the LORD, and instead of coming with praise he brings his doubts. Listen to the opening words of Habakkuk:

> How long, LORD, must I call for help, but you do not listen? Or cry out to you, "Violence!" but you do not save? Why do you make me look at injustice? Why do you tolerate wrongdoing? Destruction and violence are before me; there is strife, and conflict abounds. Therefore the law is paralyzed, and justice never prevails. The wicked hem in the righteous, so that justice is perverted. (Habakkuk 1:2–4 NIV)

These aren't the words we'd expect to hear from a faithful prophet. And yet, here they are. The Bible isn't blind toward the harsh realities of suffering, and it never offers a simple answer or tells people to "get over it." Habakkuk isn't alone either. David, Job, Paul, and others throughout Scripture have similar conversations with God.

In the midst of these conversations, God hears their complaints and accusations, and he responds with patience and affection. When God answers Habakkuk, it's an invitation to trust God's sovereign affection for Israel: "Look at the nations and watch—and be utterly amazed. For I am going to do something in your days that you would not believe, even if you were told" (Habakkuk 1:5 NIV). After Job has spends thirty-seven chapters questioning God and pleading for the opportunity to defend himself to God, the Lord arrives and asks Job, "Where were you when I laid the earth's foundation? Tell me, if you understand. Who marked off its dimensions? Surely you know! Who stretched a measuring line across it?" (Job 38:4–5 NIV). This type of questioning continues for a while, and it effectively reminds Job (and us!) that we're asking questions way above our pay grade when we accuse God of being indifferent toward suffering.

The Bible doesn't criticize us for asking God these questions. They're perfectly natural questions for us to ask! But, as Jesus says, "I have spoken to you of earthly things and you do not believe; how then will you believe if I speak of heavenly things?" (John 3:12 NIV) As Christians, it's important to remember the problem of suffering is never easily answered. It remains a difficult and often painful question—but what the Bible does provide is this: confidence in a sovereign God who is full of love and compassion for people to the extent that he gave his own son in order that they would be restored into a right relationship with him. If God has loved us like that, then we can trust him with our suffering.

No Simplistic Answers

Although we might believe God is trustworthy, our questions about suffering remain. On the one hand, it is entirely right and biblical to believe, "This isn't the way it's supposed to be." We know the suffering we endure simply isn't right. We were made to experience the perfect peace of Eden, yet our thumbs are pricked by thorns and we are betrayed by our own bodies. The world has been turned inside out by sin. Some Christians have become so jaded by this world they accept suffering as something that's perfectly normal. Biblically speaking, sin and death and suffering have become *imperfectly* normal in all creation. They are foreign realities in this world that will not endure into eternity.

On the other hand, we believe that God is so sovereign that he uses everything—even our suffering—to accomplish his purpose. There is great comfort in knowing "that for those who love God all things work together for good" (Romans 8:28). This verse doesn't mean we're always going to get what we want. But it does give assurance that nothing in life will be meaningless, especially our tears and pain. God will not waste a single tear. All things contribute to help us behold the love and power of God. Suffering is a reminder that this world is not the way it's supposed to be. It's a warning against living for false gods who cannot deliver on the promises they make. It's a painful reality check that death cannot be avoided, and we're only kidding ourselves if we live like we're immortal.

Sometimes suffering is clearly the result of sin (like a school shooting), and sometimes it "just happens" (like cancer). Other times it's a confusing mixture (car accidents, or a surgery gone wrong). It's okay to bring however you feel or whatever you're thinking to God in prayer. He is remarkably gentle with us, especially when we're struggling. Sometimes, the best we can ask for is peace, rather than an answer to all the "why" questions we ask. Suffering is easier to come to terms with when there's someone to blame. But moments like these invite us to lift our eyes to God—who spoke the heavens and earth into place, who sustains all things, and who will judge all creation on that final day—and to determine whether or not we can trust him despite our confusion.

Even if you have felt powerless to defend yourself in this life, you can trust that God will bring everything into the light and will give proper judgment. This is why the apostle Paul writes, "Do not take revenge, my dear friends, but leave room for God's wrath, for it is written: 'It is mine to avenge; I will repay,' says the Lord." (Romans 12:19 NIV). Everyone who cares about evil and injustice looks forward to those perpetrators coming to justice. When you have been wronged, there is great comfort in trusting God's judgment. As we already discussed in chapter six, God's judgment is actually an expression of his love. God's patience is sometimes misinterpreted as apathy. In case there is any question about God's concern over sin and evil and suffering, we only need to look to the cross.

Look to the Cross

The crucifixion and death of Jesus Christ is the greatest act of evil in human history. Think about it: God loved us so much he came into our world as a human baby who was eventually betrayed and abandoned by his friends, framed by the priests who were entrusted with the honor of leading God's people in worship, and then crucified among the vilest offenders of the day while the crowd mocked him. At the cross, we see intense suffering (the only perfectly innocent man, hung on a cross), God's holiness (Jesus was the sinless, perfect Son of God), his love (he gave himself as our substitute), his power (he would conquer death by enduring it), and his wrath (he did not overlook the judgment sin deserves, but poured it out upon Jesus). Jesus understands your suffering—not merely as a theory, but from the inside.

God's grace in suffering rings especially clear through four promises offered in Romans 8. First, we hear that God is with us and he understands our suffering, since the Son himself has come "in the likeness of sinful flesh and for sin" (v. 3). Second, the way we endure suffering shows the world we are living for another kingdom that will surely come when Christ returns: "The sufferings of this present time are not worth comparing with the glory that is to be revealed to us" (v. 18). Third, we cling to hope that God is working out his plan of salvation despite our suffering, so that "all things work together for good" (v. 28). Finally, we live with cross-shaped endurance because God issued his judgment that, "we are more than conquerors through him who loved us" (v. 37).

God doesn't leave us to suffer in a hopeless world. He entered in, took the worst this world has to offer upon his own shoulders, and he conquered it. The gospel proclaims good news because the cross isn't the end of the story. Jesus identifies with us in our guilt and in our sufferings, but he rose from the grave in victory over sin and death. The curse of sin has been defeated, and we share in that victory by faith. The gift of the gospel is truly amazing: forgiveness, adoption, eternal life, hope, joy, love, and so much more.

Even in the midst of great suffering, God's sovereignty and his goodness have not flickered, but continue to shine in their perfect brilliance, highlighting the hope we have through the empty tomb. Jesus has risen from the grave, and he will return to wipe away every tear. In the midst of our pain, Christians live with eternal hope because Jesus will finish the good work that he began.

DIGGING DEEPER

Use these questions for your own personal reflection and journaling, or for discussion with others.

- What are some ways you've learned and grown as a result of challenges and suffering in your life?
- If it were up to you, how much suffering do you think God should allow?
- What does this chapter mean by calling the crucifixion of Jesus the greatest act of evil in human history?
- How can the death, resurrection, and eventual return of Jesus Christ give you hope and endurance when you suffer?

Recommended Resources

I f this book has prompted a desire to read and study more, here are a few "next steps" for you.

RECOMMENDED BOOKS FOR YOUR FAITH

Cameron Cole and Charlotte Getz, *The Jesus I Wish I Knew in High School* (Greensboro, NC: New Growth Press, 2021)

Kevin DeYoung, *Taking God at His Word: Why the Bible Is Knowable, Necessary, and Enough, and What That Means for You and Me* (Wheaton, IL: Crossway, 2014)

Greg Gilbert, *What Is the Gospel?* (Wheaton, IL: Crossway, 2010)

Drew Hill, *Alongside Jesus: Devotions for Teenagers* (Greensboro, NC: New Growth Press, 2022)

Greg Koukl, *Tactics: A Game Plan for Discussing Your Christian Convictions, Updated and Expanded* (Grand Rapids, MI: Zondervan, 2019)

C. S. Lewis, *Mere Christianity* (New York: HarperOne, 2015)

Todd Miles, *Superheroes Can't Save You: Epic Examples of Historic Heresies* (Nashville, TN: B&H Academic, 2018)

Nate Pickowitz, *How to Eat Your Bible: A Simple Approach to Learning and Loving the Word of God* (Chicago: Moody, 2021).

Barnabas Piper, *Help My Unbelief: Why Doubt Is Not the Enemy of Faith* (Charlotte, NC: The Good Book Company, 2020)

John Stott, *Basic Christianity* (Downer's Grove, IL: IVP, 2019)

RECOMMENDED BOOKS ABOUT DIFFICULT TOPICS

Greg Gilbert, *Why Trust the Bible?* (Wheaton, IL: Crossway, 2015)

Josh McDowell and Sean McDowell, *Evidence That Demands a Verdict: Life-Changing Truth for a Skeptical World*, rev. ed. (Nashville, TN: Thomas Nelson, 2017)

Rebecca McLaughlin, *Confronting Christianity: 12 Hard Questions for the World's Largest Religion* (Wheaton, IL: Crossway, 2019)

Rebecca McLaughlin, *10 Questions Every Teen Should Ask (and Answer) about Christianity* (Wheaton, IL: Crossway, 2021)

David Murray, *Why Am I Feeling Like This?: A Teen's Guide to Freedom from Anxiety and Depression* (Wheaton, IL: Crossway, 2020)

RECOMMENDED BOOKS ABOUT CHRISTIAN SEXUALITY

Kevin DeYoung, *What Does the Bible Really Teach about Homosexuality?* (Wheaton, IL: Crossway, 2015)

Rachel Gilson, *Born Again This Way: Coming Out, Coming to Faith, and What Comes Next* (Charlotte, NC: The Good book Company, 2020)

Heath Lambert, *Finally Free: Fighting for Purity with the Power of Grace* (Grand Rapids, MI: Zondervan, 2013)

Jackie Hill Perry, *Good God, Gay Girl: The Story of Who I Was, and Who God Has Always Been* (Nashville, TN: B&H Books, 2018)

Preston Sprinkle, *Embodied: Transgender Identities, the Church, and What the Bible Has to Say* (Colorado Springs, CO: David C. Cook, 2021).

Preston Sprinkle, *Living in a Gray World: A Christian Teen's Guide to Understanding Homosexuality* (Grand Rapids, MI: Zondervan, 2015)

Endnotes

Chapter 2

1. Dietrich Bonhoeffer, *The Cost of Discipleship* (New York: Touchstone, 1995), 45.

Chapter 3

1. Greg Gilbert, *Why Trust the Bible?* (Wheaton, IL: Crossway, 2015). This is a short book and an easy first step to further study of the historical reliability of the Bible.

2. Josh McDowell and Sean McDowell, *Evidence That Demands a Verdict: Life-Changing Truth for a Skeptical World*, rev. ed. (Nashville, TN: Thomas Nelson, 2017), 52.

3. McDowell and McDowell, *Evidence*, 52.

4. F. F. Bruce, *The Canon of Scripture*, 2nd. ed. (Downers Grove, IL: IVP Academic, 2018). Section Four especially deals with the issues of how the Early Church identified books to be included in the Bible. *Evidence That Demands a Verdict* also has multiple helpful chapters about the formation of the Bible, its trustworthiness, and other "gnostic gospels" that are not considered biblical.

Chapter 5

1. Barnabas Piper, *Help My Unbelief: Why Doubt Is Not the Enemy of Faith* (The Good Book Company, 2020), 81–90.

Chapter 6

1. Kevin Yi, "Death to Life in the Heart of Leadership" (Message presented at the Rooted Conference, Dallas, TX, 10/27/17).

Chapter 8

1. Most famously, see Tacitus's *Annals* 14.44 and Josephus's *Antiquities* 18.3.3.

Chapter 11

1. Aaron Earls, "Most Teenagers Drop Out of Church as Young Adults," Lifeway Research, January 15, 2019, https://life wayresearch.com/2019/01/15/most-teenagers-drop-out-of-church-as-young-adults/.

Chapter 14

1. Fight the New Drug, "Teens Watch Porn to Learn About Sex—This Is What Porn Teaches Them." August 11, 2022, https://fightthenewdrug.org/these-3-studies-show-how-pornography-is-affecting-teens/.

Chapter 15

1. The Barna Group, *Gen Z: The Culture, Beliefs and Motivations Shaping the Next Generation* (Ventura, CA: Barna Group, 2018), 46–47.

2. Jeffrey M. Jones, "LGBT Identification in U.S. Ticks Up to 7.1%," Gallup, February 17, 2022, https://news.gallup.com/poll/389792/lgbt-identification-ticks-up.aspx.

3. Preston Sprinkle, *Embodied: Transgender Identities, the Church, and What the Bible Has to Say* (Colorado Springs, CO: David C. Cook, 2021).

4. Abigail Shrierer, *Irreversible Damage: The Transgender Craze Seducing Our Daughters* (Washington D.C.: Regnery Publishing, 2021).

5. Here are two books to read to learn more: Preston Sprinkle, *Embodied: Transgender Identities, the Church, and What the Bible Has to Say* (Colorado Springs, CO: David C. Cook, 2021); and Abigail

Shrierer, *Irreversible Damage: The Transgender Craze Seducing Our Daughters* (Washington D.C.: Regnery Publishing, 2021).

Chapter 16

1. For more on adaptation and evolution within species, see Jonathan Sarfati, *Refuting Evolution: A Handbook for Students, Parents, and Teachers Countering the Latest Arguments for Evolution* (Atlanta, GA: Creation Book Publishers, 2008).

2. This view is most famously presented by Meredith G. Kline in *Kingdom Prologue: Genesis Foundations for a Covenantal Worldview* (Eugene, OR: Wipf and Stock, 2006).

Chapter 17

1. Juliana Menasce Horowitz and Nikki Graf, "Most U.S. Teens See Anxiety and Depression as a Major Problem Among Their Peers," Pew Research Center, February 20, 2019, https://www.pewsocialtrends.org/2019/02/20/most-u-s-teens-see-anxiety-and-depression-as-a-major-problem-among-their-peers/.